Planning, for a Change

A citizen's guide to creative planning and program development

Duane Dale and Nancy Mitiguy
of the Citizen Involvement Training
Project (CITP)

Editing: Robbie Gordon
Design: Ann McCaffrey
Layout: Meg Davenport
Graphics: Ann McCaffrey
          Meg Davenport

© **University of Massachusetts (Citizen Involvement Training Project) 1978**

The Citizen Involvement Training Project (CITP) is a collaborative
project of the Division of Continuing Education and the Cooperative
Extension Service at the University of Massachusetts at Amherst.
CITP is funded by a major grant from the W.K. Kellogg Foundation
of Battle Creek, Michigan, with additional support from the Blan-
chard and Polaroid Foundations. Portions of this manual were prepared under contract with the Massachusetts Bicentennial Commission for use during its **Citizencraft** project.

Our thanks to the citizen group members whose descriptions of
their program-planning efforts are included in this manual:

Ellen Cassedy of Nine to Five, Boston, Mass.

**Frances Crowe of the American Friends Service Committee and
Mobilization for Survival, Northampton, Mass.**

Pat Sackrey of Women in Agriculture, Northampton, Mass.

Their commentaries are a testimony to the thoughtfulness
with which some groups already approach program development.

Our thanks also to the reviewers of this manual:

**Jack Wilson, Vice President, Board of Directors, Franklin-Hampshire
Community Mental Health Center, Amherst, Mass.**

Esther Calish, Director, Beverly Public Library, Beverly, Mass.

George Schaler, Director, Agawam Youth Center, Agawam, Mass.

Their recommendations were consistently well-reasoned and were
almost always heeded; any remaining shortcomings are, of course,
the responsibility of the authors.

ISBN 0-934210-01-2

Library of Congress Catalog Card Number: 79-624733

Table of Contents

INTRODUCTIONS

1 OVERVIEW OF PLANNING

2 RATE YOUR GROUP'S PLANNING PROCESS

3 GETTING STARTED

4 GENERATING PROGRAM IDEAS

5 CHOOSING A PROGRAM

6 STRATEGIES: MAKING PROGRAMS HAPPEN

7 EVALUATION

8 RESOURCES

Introductions

The Citizen Involvement Training Project

The Citizen Involvement Training Project (CITP) is a three-year project of the Division of Continuing Education and the Cooperative Extension Service. Funded by the W.K. Kellogg Foundation, CITP provides training workshops, materials, and consultations to citizen groups throughout Massachusetts. The staff of nine includes specialists in organizing, fund-raising, group process, planning methods, information gathering, social change and adult education, and offers bilingual training as well.

CITP services include workshops and consultation, a 1000 volume Citizen Involvement Library (available to individuals and citizen groups), staff-generated manuals (such as this) and a "Training of Trainers" workshop series intended to help citizen groups establish their own training components in their communities.

Citizen Involvement Training Project
Division of Continuing Education
University of Massachusetts
Amherst, Mass. 01003

(413) 545-3450

About Citizen "Training"

The word "training" may bring to mind a lion trainer, or a sergeant drilling an army—the sort of learning where one person is in charge and the trainee is in a passive or submissive role. "On-the-job training" brings forth a different image, however—that of a worker learning new skills relevant to the job she is about to begin. Citizen Involvement Training is, more precisely, on-the-job training . . . since all of us are full-time citizens (though few of us received formal education in the field and fewer receive the benefits).

Citizen Involvement Training consists of people learning how to identify and then acquire the skills they need as citizen group members in order to take the next step toward success. Ideally, it is _active_ learning, since people do not tend to learn to be more powerful by taking a passive role in the learning process. So the "curricula" for citizens who want to have a say in decision-making (as CITP approaches it) consists of role-plays and simulations, diagnostic interviews and checklists, small-group discussions centered around specific relevant issues, or perhaps simply providing the encouragement a group needs to go out and do something—consciously—with feedback and evaluation from CITP staff and citizen group members.

About the CITP Manual Series

Usually, when CITP conducts a workshop for a citizen group, CITP staff members first sit down with the group to diagnose the problems and needs. The diagnostic sessions consist of probing questions which are aimed at helping the group identify root causes as well as immediate, readily apparent needs. Many groups come in feeling that they need help with fund-raising, only to find that the need for funds is a symptom of a deeper problem -- perhaps a poor goal-setting or decision-making structure, or management style. Some groups think they need help writing better press releases and discover some interpersonal problems which stand in the way of effecting a coordinated media effort.

After diagnosing the problems and needs, the CITP staff and representatives of the group or agency then sit down to design a workshop or workshop series to suit those needs.

This manual, as well as others in the series, is intended to help citizen groups set up their own on-the-job training activities, tailored to their own individual needs, issues, learning styles and experiences. In writing these guides we have used what we have learned through our experience with hundreds of citizen groups to help you ask yourselves questions which will tap both universal and unique citizen group problems.

POWER: A
REPOSSESION
MANUAL

. . .a manual for organizers and
members of community
organizations:

Those citizen group members who
have participated in a CITP
workshop (or some other training
workshop) will be able to use the
manuals as a back-home resource to continue personal skill-
building or to share it with others.
Activities and information described
in the manuals, however, have also
been geared for those who have
never had personal contact with
CITP.

It is also hoped that these manuals
will be used to help orient new
members to an organization, and
will be an integral part of
membership/staff development.
Some organizations are reluctant
to spend time on training activities,
at least at first, before the merits
have been proven. The reluctance
is appropriate: training can be a
diversion from the real concerns
of the group. But training activities
can focus so directly on those
"real concerns" that progress
toward more long-range goals is
made during the training; doing
and learning can become almost
indistinguishable.

If you are the one introducing
training exercises to your group,
you might want to first spend
some time discussing these
reluctances or individual
learning preferences. Then again,
you may want to let the proof
of the pudding rest in the
tasting.

About the Exercises

There are several exercises
and sections in this manual which
you might want to duplicate,
reorder to suit your group's
needs or use as a smaller, con-
densed version of a "training
workbook" for the entire group.

Whatever way you use the manual,
we hope you will tailor it to
suit your own needs and learning
style. All exercises in the manual
have been formated on single
pages so that you can duplicate
them easily; exercises are denoted
as such so that you will know
they are optional as you read
through each chapter. You may
want to read through the entire
manual first, before trying the
exercises. On the other hand
many people find that the information in the manual has more
relevance after they do the exercises.

About the Use of He, She, etc.

While trying to avoid the inherent
male bias in our current English
language, we have run up against
the cumbersome problem of having
to break up the flow of a sentence
or train of thought by saying "he/she,
him/herself."

We have therefore opted instead to
alternate the gender of the personal
pronoun throughout the body of
the manual. This is not a stylistic
mistake, it was intentional. It is
hoped that our culture will devise
appropriate pronouns in the future
to compensate for the problems
currently presented authors and
editors (not to mention men and
women).

How to Use This Manual

- read it cover-to-cover;
- read the parts that seem most relevant to your group's situation;
- skip the reading and go straight to the sets of questions and the activities;
- treat it as a guide for back-home learning activities.

The following summary will help you decide which parts may be most useful to you:

As a self-study guide, this booklet can be used as you choose — start wherever you want, pick the activity which seems to serve your needs. It's your tool for better planning. The introductions to each section will help you find the most useful pages.

Why are You Doing This to Yourself?

(Objective Setting)

Unless you've been chained to the wall with this manual thrust under your nose, you obviously *chose* to look through this material on program planning. Please explain yourself.

What specific skills or concepts do you hope to learn from this manual?

-
-
-
-
-

Congratulations! You've just finished one step in the planning process: a statement of objectives.

In this case, you've written (hopefully) some specifics about what *you* need or would like to learn about program planning. Compare your objectives with the table of contents, and it should be easy to identify the pages and sections that will be most useful to you.

The best is yet to come.

1

Overview of Planning

The purpose of this manual is to give you a "bag of tricks" for planning. Remember the black leather bags that doctors used to take on house calls? (Do you remember when doctors used to make house calls?) Imagine the tangle of tools if those big bags had no compartments. In this section, we'll give you some "compartments" to help you sort out the planning tools coming up.

What is Planning?

Planning is a sequence of steps, a method of getting to your goal, a "recipe" for group action, an image of the future as you hope it will unfold.

"All we ever do is talk. I want to see some action."

Every group has spokespeople for that position, and rightly so. But good planning is more than "just talk." Here are some of the things you can hope to accomplish with a careful plan:

Clarify choices: You'll know what paths you *didn't* choose from the start and can avoid having one-third of the group split ranks mid-way through a project and decide that "we'd rather hold a bazaar." Put it another way: If you consider several different program ideas and check member interest in each, you'll know how committed people are from the beginning.

Let everyone know what happens next: This keeps individuals "plugging away" and provides a basis for teamwork.

Avoid or anticipate difficulties: Shortages of money, uncooperative local officials, and bad weather are a few of the problems that can plague good programs. Planning can help you anticipate, avoid, or work around them.

Provide inspiration: Everyone knows that the sequence of activities (no matter how complicated or difficult) is leading toward a goal that is important to the group. The plan becomes a source of inspiration, by providing the assurance that "it's all going someplace."

Product and Process

When architects plan buildings, they are designing (planning) a *product* (the structure we will see) and also planning the construction *process*. If the process is a conventional one, we don't think much about it; we assume that the building can be built because we have seen so many other steel and glass skyscrapers or brick homes or whatever. But if the architect's sketch shows a roof of rippling, free-form concrete — like nothing we ever saw before — we want to know whether it can be built. "How will you do that?"

Perhaps we listen with skepticism as the architect explains: "I will mound earth with bulldozers, then lay down steel reinforcing rods, and pour the concrete over them. Then I will dig the earth out from under the roof." The architect has specified a sequence of steps — a *process* — which she thinks (or hopes) will lead to the desired *product*.

Social action projects often choose unconventional goals. One of the things we accomplish by planning is to make sure there's a *workable* process for achieving those goals.

PROCESS... THE STEPS TO A PRODUCT!

"Models" of the Planning Process

The "Model" is where we provide the mental "storage compartments" for the planning tools that will follow. We're using "model" in the sense of an *example* - an outline to follow, an image of how the planning process might proceed. There are any number of possible procedures and combinations of procedures, though many of them have similarities. We'll present three, and you can decide which version you like best.

MODEL NUMBER 1: A BASIC PROGRAM-PLANNING MODEL

This approach is based on the outline that foundation and government funding proposals often recommend or require, namely:

- State project *Goals and Objectives*
- State *Methods* (project description)
- Specify *Implementation Procedure*
- Specify *Evaluation Procedure*

That's fine for a proposal outline, but since we need to be more concerned about how the program is developed, we would expand the outline to one more like the model on the right.

- Identify needs of community and organization
- Review organization's purposes and goals
- Reconcile needs with goals

→ State project *Goals and Objectives*

- Develop alternative program ideas
- Assess desirability and feasibility
- Select best program method

→ State *Methods* (project description)

- Develop detailed plan, contingency plan, staffing, pattern, time-line, etc.

→ Specify *Implementation Procedure*

- Determine evaluation criteria
- Select data-gathering process
- Develop evaluation questions

→ Specify *Evaluation Procedure*

MODEL NUMBER 2: A PROBLEM-SOLVING APPROACH

This model is typical of the approach followed by organizations that train people in problem-solving and creative thinking. It can be applied to program design and also to troubleshooting when you have a program in operation that isn't up to par.

There are several bits of wisdom — problem-solving principles — which provide the cornerstones of this approach:

- Problems aren't always what they seem to be at first glance. The way you state the problem directs your attention to one type of solution or another, so it's important to play with different wordings of the problem and discover which seem most fruitful.

- No *one* method can be guaranteed to lead to a solution. Sometimes it helps to clarify the ideal (goal); sometimes it helps to state what the present situation is; sometimes it helps to explore different interpretations of "What causes this problem?"

- There is probably no such thing as a *totally* new idea. For instance, the pocket calulator is an invention that puts together several earlier inventions, such as the integrated circuit chip and the light-emitting-diode display. So: once you have refined your problem statement, it's useful to inventory the existing methods or inventions that may contribute to a solution. You will still be faced with the creative challenge of combining ideas into a new product or program — perhaps unlike anything that has ever been tried before.

- The first solution is rarely the best. Generate lots of possible solutions, then choose several for refinement.

With these principles as background, consider this version of the problem-solving process to the right.*

In this manual, we draw on the problem-solving approach as a way of generating program ideas. In other words, we build parts of model number 2 into model number 1.

Problem-Solving Process	*Example*
1. State problem situation in broad terms.	*Organization has no money in treasury.*
2. Analyze the nature and causes of the problem situation.	*No dues; no fund-raising events; inflation caused cost overrun on last project.*
3. Describe ideal situation . . . and present situation.	*Ideal: $2,000 in bank; adequate money for next project.* *Present: No money; projects not being developed because they don't seem affordable.*
4. State alternative versions of the problem.	*No money; projects aren't being developed; morale is low; opportunities are being missed.*
5. Choose one version of the problem (or a combination) to pursue.	*Opportunities are being missed because morale is low, and therefore new projects are not being developed.*
6. Inventory existing solutions.	*Hold fund-raising events; develop low-budget or zero-budget projects, identify opportunities and decide how to pursue them (should also build morale); ask the group, "What would we be doing if we had $2,000 in the bank?"*
7. Generate new solutions (probably a synthesis of existing solutions).	*Hold an organizational meeting to explore opportunities, low-budget project ideas, etc. (mixture of strategies from step number 6).*
8. State guidelines for choosing ("decision criteria") and select best solution.	*We want activities which will bring in money and encourage people to get acquainted, so we'll hold a benefit dinner-dance.*
9. Implement and document.	*Do it! Keep a log, journal or up-dated time-line to keep track of the process and its progress.*

*For more information on this problem-solving approach, see the book, **Universal Traveler**, by Don Koberg and Jim Bagnall (Resource Section, page 85).

MODEL NUMBER 3:
THE 4-STROKE INTERNAL
COMBUSTION ENGINE
APPROACH

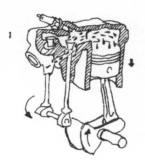

Finally, just to demonstrate that any sort of "model" can shed some light on the planning process, consider the ways that planning processes are like the four strokes of a gasoline engine:

Intake: Information is taken in about the problems, needs, goals, objectives, resources, and existing strategies. Just as the combustion chamber is expanding, so also are the ideas under consideration in this planning stage.

Compression: The combustible materials are compressed, or perhaps "digested," into usable form. There is an attempt to *narrow* the amount of information into useful summaries, eliminating that which is extraneous.

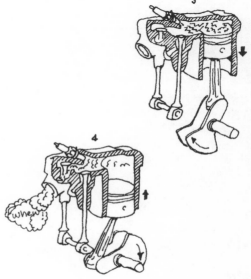

Ignition: Something new is generated from the ingredients: energy from the engine, program ideas from the planning process (again, the ideas are expanding).

Exhaust: This is a narrowing stage. The piston is moving in the engine, driving out the exhaust gases. And at this point in the planning process, the group is choosing from among its options, narrowing things down to the best program option, and perhaps preparing to repeat the four-step cycle on the level of detailed implementation steps.

In short, the process of inventing and choosing program options can be seen as one of alternately expanding and narrowing the group's thinking.

The next section presents some ways to assess your group's present planning process. After you do so, you may want to return to the three models just described and consider the following questions:

- *Which of the three models is closest to the way we plan now?*

- *Which of these describes the way I would like us to plan?* You may find that what you're

after is a mixture of ingredients—something from each of the three models.

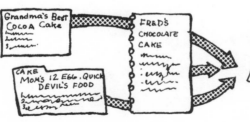

- What is your group's planning process now?

- How well does your group plan?

- Who should be involved in planning?

- What are your group's present commitments and activites?

2

Rate Your Group's Planning Process

At this point it's helpful to take stock of how your group currently plans now and how effective the process is for you. The exercises in this section correspond to the four basic questions above.

The final activity of the section is a stimulated planning process which will give you a chance to think about your own role in the process and will provide a basis for discussions about good planning.

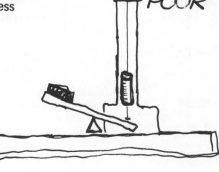

What is Your Group's Planning Process Now?

no. people: one to several
minimum time: 40 minutes
Materials: copies of questionaires below

Now that you've seen some examples of different planning processes, you may want to compare then with how your organization plans. That may not be an easy task, since planning doesn't occur in neat, distinct steps. It's helpful, however, to try to make some generalizations about how your group plans so you can then determine how well you plan.

This exercise can be either an individual or a group activity. It may be useful to include other members of your organization if there appears to be some confusion or resentment about the role of planning in the organization.

1. Each person who is participating in the activity should receive a copy of the chart below and spend ten minutes or so filling it out.

2. This information can then be shared with other group members, either by passing out copies of each person's chart, by making brief verbal statements, or by summarizing the comments on newsprint.

3. The group may want to spend 20-30 minutes discussing why it plans the way it does and/or making comparisons to the planning models in this booklet.

Who does the planning in your organization? (Circle your choice)	*When is the planning done in your organization? (Circle your choices, or add some of your own)*	*What's the step-by-step process you use to plan programs? (Put a number beside each item, indicating which step is usually done first, second, third, etc.)*
Program participants	Once a year	Conduct a needs survey
Volunteers	Every week	Ask people for ideas about possible programs
Board of directors	Monthly	Make a time-line
Advisory board	Never	Determine the organization's goals
Committees	At annual weekend retreats	Choose specific program activities
Staff	At community-wide meetings	Evaluate present activities
Funding source(s)	Covertly (i.e., no one knows)	Figure out what your resources are
Other:	Other:	Enlist support from the community

4. Now use a different color pen (or boxes instead of circles) to indicate how you think the group *should* plan.

5. The statements below describe different aspects of the planning process. There are four possible answers to each: agree, disagree, neutral or don't know. Circle the answer which fits *your opinion* of how the group operates.

1. The group spends too much time planning.	agree	disagree	neutral	don't know
2. An appropriate number of people are involved in planning.	agree	disagree	neutral	don't know
3. The group has a clear, workable plan for major activities.	agree	disagree	neutral	don't know
4. The group's activities relate to stated goals and purposes.	agree	disagree	neutral	don't know
5. The group knows what it will be doing two years from now.	agree	disagree	neutral	don't know
6. The group is good at coming up with creative program possibilities.	agree	disagree	neutral	don't know
7. The group is able to choose one course of action and stick to it.	agree	disagree	neutral	don't know

6. You might want to circulate copies of this list to others in your group and ask them to answer the questions. Major discrepancies in responses could mean that the function of planning is not understood by everyone in your group or that there are some holes in the planning process your group uses now.

7. A quick way to compare responses once you're back in a large group, is to ask how many people disagreed with each item. A show of hands will tell you which aspects of the planning process need further discussion and improvement.

Discussion Questions

- *If you disagreed with one of the seven statements, why?*

- *What needs to be done to improve the group's planning process?*

- *What parts of the planning process are we doing right?*

Who Should Be Involved in Planning?

no. people: one to several
minimum time: 25 minutes
materials: paper and pen

A first step is to determine who could potentially be involved in planning, both from within and outside the organization. Here are some general groupings:

Steering Committee
Publicity Committee
Volunteers
Advisory Board
Planning Committee
Board of Directors
Members

Government agencies
Local community
Potential program participants
Business
Politicians
Churches
Foundations

Membership Committee
Staff
Personnel Committee
Program participants
Media
Other citizen groups

1. Take five minutes and develop your own list, identifying *specific* groups (or individuals) in your community who should be involved. In the spirit of citizen participation, your list should include everyone who is directly or indirectly affected by your decisions. If the list is long, you don't necessarily have to eliminate people from your planning process. One way to narrow the field of potential planners is to figure out who should be involved in the various levels of planning; some might be less involved than others. Consider these questions: Who will be affected most by the planning decisions? Do these people have the time, energy, and desire to participate?

2. It may be helpful to convert your list into a diagram, with those you think should be most involved in planning near the middle. It might look like this:

People who should be involved in Planning a new Multipurpose Center for Senior Citizens

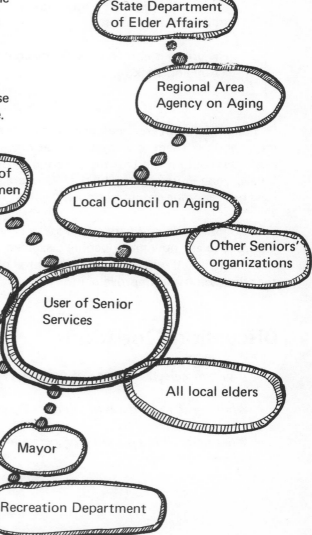

22

How Well Does Your Group Plan?

There are many ways of determining the effectiveness of your group's planning process. Here are some activities that you could do on your own or with other members of your group.

- Find out how satisfied members/participants are with the program (personal interview, group discussions, surveys).

- Make a list of all the programs conducted by your group during the past year. Which were successful? Which could have been improved and how? Which were discontinued? Why?

- Videotape the group's planning sessions. Replay it to the members, and ask for general comments about how well the process worked and suggestions for improvement.

- Keep a personal diary of planning decisions. Review the diary at the end of each month, and assess the progress your group is making in implementing its planning decisions.

- Compare the *results* of past programs to the organization's stated purpose and goals. Did each program relate directly to the goals and objectives? How much closer are you to achieving the group's goals as a result of each program?

- List the things your group will be doing in three years. If you can't, a long-range planning session may be appropriate.

What are Your Present Commitments and Activities?

no. people: one - 15 people
minimum time: 15 minutes
materials: newsprint, felt-tipped markers

One of the purposes of planning is to make decisions about programs and activities. Let's explore the planning decisions you as a group have already made during the last year.

1. Spend about 15 minutes filling in the chart below. Ask each member of the group to do the same.

2. Share the information by incorporating everyone's comments into one listing.

Projects/activities the group is committed to	Date project will end	Project ideas discussed but not discarded	Major policy decisions

Discussion Questions

1. Are there projects which should be scaled down or eliminated because they no longer reflect the group's priorities?

2. How much time and energy are available for new projects?

3. Is your group able to sustain several projects at once or is it more effective when the entire group focuses its energies on one thing.

4. What policies or ideas are not being fully implemented that should be?

A Small Dose of Planning

no. people: 6 to many
minimum time: 20 minutes
materials: newsprint, felt pens

What is the "ideal" planning process? You could begin to answer that question by reading what other people have to say about the various steps involved in planning programs. Or you can extract from your own experience the process that has worked best for you.

Another method that generates creative thinking and discussion is to begin with a simple "planning exercise" like the one below. This will provide all members of the group with a common frame of reference for a discussion and critique of the many ways of planning.

1. Divide into groups of 6 people. Read the planning exercise below.

2. Select one person from each group to keep the discussion moving and another person to record *how* the group plans (i.e., a chronological sequence of decisions). The recorder will later share your group's planning process with other workshop participants.

3. With your group, come up with a plan for one of the situations below:

SITUATION #1:

You are a member of the local Conservation Commisison. The primary purpose of the commission is to preserve and protect the natural resources and environment of the town. At last evening's commission meeting, there was considerable discussion about the lack of communication between the commission and the community. You and a few other commission members agreed to come up with a strategy to increase communication. It won't be an easy task because there is no money in the budget for this effort and you have only 20 minutes to plan a strategy. *Why, what, how* and *when* questions might be appropriate for your committee to think about.

SITUATION #2:

You and some energetic members of your group have volunteered to plan the annual fund-raising event. During the next 20 minutes, you and they will plan all the details. You might want to think about such things as specific activities, logistics, purpose. Keep it simple because you have only 20 minutes.

4. Now compare what you've just done in this planning exercise with the four steps in an "ideal" planning process

5. Compare what you've done in this planning exercise with Planning Model 1

Discussion Questions

You might want to use the following as the basis for a post-exercise discussion:

- *Which steps did your group spend the most time on?*

- *Would it have been better to spend more time on earlier steps? later steps?*

- *How did you go about generating methods for dealing with the situations?*

- *How many different program ideas (methods, strategies) did you generate? Would you have done better to generate more options—or to move on to the details of implementing your plan?*

- *Would you say that there is agreement or disagreement within your group about the underlying problem you were trying to deal with in this situation? Did you spend any time exploring the nature of the problem?*

- *How do you know when to stop generating ideas?*

- Does your group have a shared understanding of the nature of the problems you're trying to deal with?

- What can you personally do to raise the level of awareness about root causes?

- How can you identify root causes?

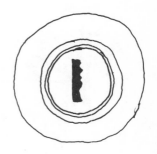

3
Getting Started

One way to get started on program planning is to clarify some of the assumptions that have gone into any previous programs your group has undertaken, and to develop your analysis of the problems you're trying to deal with. To help you explore this route, here are two exercises which can be used by either individuals or groups. The first is a question-and-answer approach; the second involves "mapping" some of the forces that influence your group and its projects.

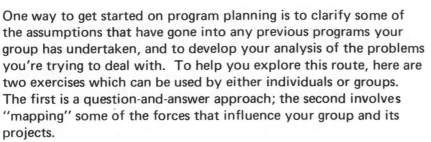

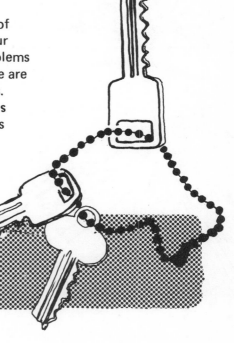

Developing Your Analysis

Rare is the group which has articulated—much less written down—its own view of the problems it's grappling with. Such theorizing strikes many people as a luxury or a waste of time; "thoughtful analysis" may conjure images of an Arnold Toynbee or some other history professor, sitting by a fireplace, contemplating the course of human events. Imagine instead an animated, informal discussion about the causes of community problems. Your community. Its problems. And your citizen group. What would it take to get that sort of process going? Perhaps the following questions would be useful for openers:

Questions for Determining Root Causes of Problems that Concern Your Group:

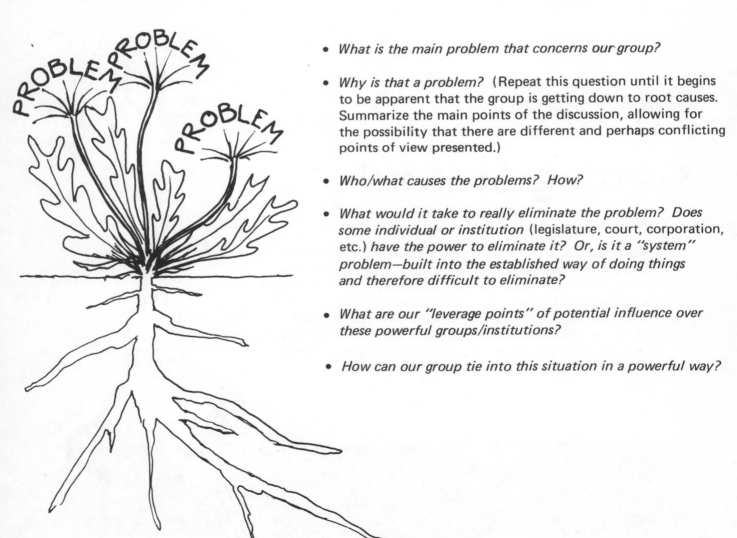

- *What is the main problem that concerns our group?*

- *Why is that a problem?* (Repeat this question until it begins to be apparent that the group is getting down to root causes. Summarize the main points of the discussion, allowing for the possibility that there are different and perhaps conflicting points of view presented.)

- *Who/what causes the problems? How?*

- *What would it take to really eliminate the problem? Does some individual or institution* (legislature, court, corporation, etc.) *have the power to eliminate it? Or, is it a "system" problem—built into the established way of doing things and therefore difficult to eliminate?*

- *What are our "leverage points" of potential influence over these powerful groups/institutions?*

- *How can our group tie into this situation in a powerful way?*

The case example below will provide a chance to try out these questions (or you may want to deal directly with your own group's program).

CASE EXAMPLE:

A local church group has been running an assistance program for migrant farm laborers at nearby farms. Recycled clothing is dropped off early in the harvest season as a gift to the laborers and their families. Canned goods and staples, such as powered milk, are delivered weekly—donations from church members. Also, the church's movie projector is loaned to the migrant camp for their weekly recreation night. (Films borrowed through the regional library system are shown.) Occasionally, church members will go to the recreation nights and talk with the migrant families.

DISCUSSION:

The church has chosen a specific program based on their own analysis of the problem. What would you say their analysis of the problem is? What is your analysis of the problem? How much of the real problem does the church's program deal with? What would happen is the program ended?

What are the church's assumptions about the "needy"? What could be done to increase the effectiveness of the program? What would you do if you were a member of the church, to raise these questions?

CASE HISTORY: AN ANALYSIS THAT WORKED

It makes sense to ask whether a thorough analysis will really be worth the group's time, whether it will really make a difference in the quality or effectiveness of the program that results. The case described here is one in which analysis really paid off; it's from the experience of **Women in Agriculture**, a small study and action group based in Northampton, Massachusetts. **Pat Sackrey** was the spokesperson for the group:

Analysis of current facts and trends

Information-gathering

We started working on the New England Small Farm Institute because we discovered that one of the huge gaps in the Massachusetts agriculture picture was the education of farmers. People who grow up on farms are tending not to stay on them as farmers; the average age of farmers in New England is 55 to 60 and there aren't any young farmers coming up to take their place.

We were concerned about the loss of farmland; we were convinced that the best way to keep land in farming was to keep farmers farming, and there weren't any coming up. We investigated here at UMass and discovered that the University teaches people how corn grows but not how to grow corn. And it was no wonder then that people weren't coming into the field. If you didn't grow up on a farm there wasn't any place to learn it from scratch, you know—at any rate,, not as a person over college age. (There are some good high school programs.)

So we decided that we wanted somebody to start educating farmers and, to make a long story short, after we investigated and found out that nobody wanted to, we decided, well heck, we'd do it ourselves. So through some very fortuitous contacts, we learned that it would be possible to perhaps do—to start a small farm school at the Belchertown State School for Retarded Citizens' old farmstead.

Taking the initiative

Identifying resources

More analysis

. . . One of our big ideas was that state-owned land which is not now being farmed is very vulnerable to development, and that there should be a lot of good uses it could be put to and we would like to be the guinea pigs. There's no precedent for a private group using such a place as Belchertown [State School]. And that's been the hardest part—working with various bureaucracies and trying to reach agreement.

Lining up support

. . . We started right away, seeing what we would need at a small farm school, and we developed a pretty comprehensive program over about a year-and-a-half, by meeting with people from everywhere, learning what we could, getting consultants in on a free basis from various agencies, to look at the soil, to talk with us about the needs for farmers who want to farm in small ways (that is, appropriate to the New England landscape) and also in energy-conserving ways—petrochemically based fertilizers and pesticides used little or not at all—the idea being that we really do have to have more self-reliance, and that that's another way we're dependent on the outside regions in some fairly scarey dimensions, is through these petrochemical inputs.

. . . We've had very good support for the project, but it's been slow; it's been two years, almost, that we've been working on it, and we are just now at the point of getting the land.

Developing Your Anaylsis:
A Sample of Analytic Thinking

The problem:

Many people in our community live in sub-standard housing—perhaps as many as 15%.

Possible Causes:

1. These people are too poor to afford any better.

2. Housing officials turn their backs on code violations.

3. Landlords are going for immediate profits without concerning themselves with building maintenance.

4. Banks have "redlined" certain neighborhoods —written them off as bad risks—so that improvement loans are not available.

This list of possible causes focuses attention on the question of "Who to blame" or rather "Who should we go to, to get some leverage on the problem?" If you pick cause #4, you may decide to try to get bankers to change their policies; if you pick cause #2, you may try to put some pressure on local government for code enforcement.

But even after you've decided to focus on one of the causes from the list above, you may still have more analysis left to do. For example, suppose you're concerned about #1 above -- the low incomes of people living in substandard housing. What is the cause of that? Some people think that the poor are basically lazy and could be making more money if they would only try harder. Others point to the need for job training programs, still others point to the way unemployment and underemployment are built into our economic system (economic planners assume that a certain percent of the population has to be unemployed in order to hold down inflation).

In other words, is the problem with the individual, with the lack of training programs, or with the economic system? Any citizen action group needs to make a choice before it can work effectively on this issue.

Even after you've reached consensus about causes, you may still have choices to make about strategy. If you've decided to work on cause #4, do you attempt to influence the bankers, or do you try to go around them by locating alternate sources of capital for improvements? There are ideas later in this manual about choosing a program approach approach; for now the question should be "What information about the banking system would we need to gather in order to be prepared to assess our chances?"

Discussion Questions

- *For the problem which concerns you, what are some possible explanations of the reasons for the problem?*

- *How do you choose among competing explanations?*

- *What factual information will be relevant?*

- *What can you do when members of your group disagree about explanations?*

- *How could you personally raise these analysis questions during the meetings and day-to-day functioning of your group?*

Force-Field Analysis

Kurt Lewin, a social psychologist, developed the notion that people and organizations operate in a "field" of forces—positive and negative influences—which affect the likelihood of achieving one's goals.

For example, a team of climbers headed for the peak of Mt. Everest might map out the various forces they had to deal with in the following way:

Negative Forces

- the cold
- thin air (difficulty breathing)
- dangers (falling, etc.)

Positive Forces

- good equipment
- maps and charts
- past experiences climbing

BRRR!

"Force-field analysis" provides a graphic summary of the direction and extent of these forces. For a citizen group, force-field analysis if a way for the group to identify "restraining" (negative) forces and "supporting" (positive) forces, evaluate the possible strengths of each, and to decide what can be done to maximize the supporting forces and minimize the restraining ones.

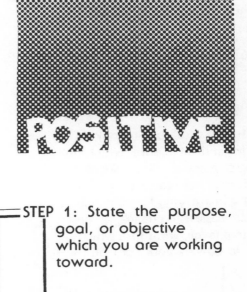

The whole organization might get involved in the force-field process, or a small sub-group, or perhaps an individual—but a variety of perspectives really helps with this one. It won't seem easy the first time through, so plan to give it at least an hour.

Force-field analysis can actually be helpful at several points in the planning process:

- during analysis, as a way to decide "what you are up against."

- during "idea generation", when trying to decide on new and innovative programs (since mapping out the positive and negative forces can suggest directions).

- as a way of choosing a program, because a "map" of forces may help you decide whether you have the resources necessary to overcome restraining forces and succeed.

It's time to lay out the steps and provide an example. Note that each step provides some useful information whether or not you go on to complete the rest of the process.

STEP 1: State the purpose, goal, or objective which you are working toward.

This may be the broadest purpose of your organization, or an objective on the way to a specific program, depending on how far your planning has progressed. Also identify the present situation. The group's problem is how to move from the present situation toward the goal.

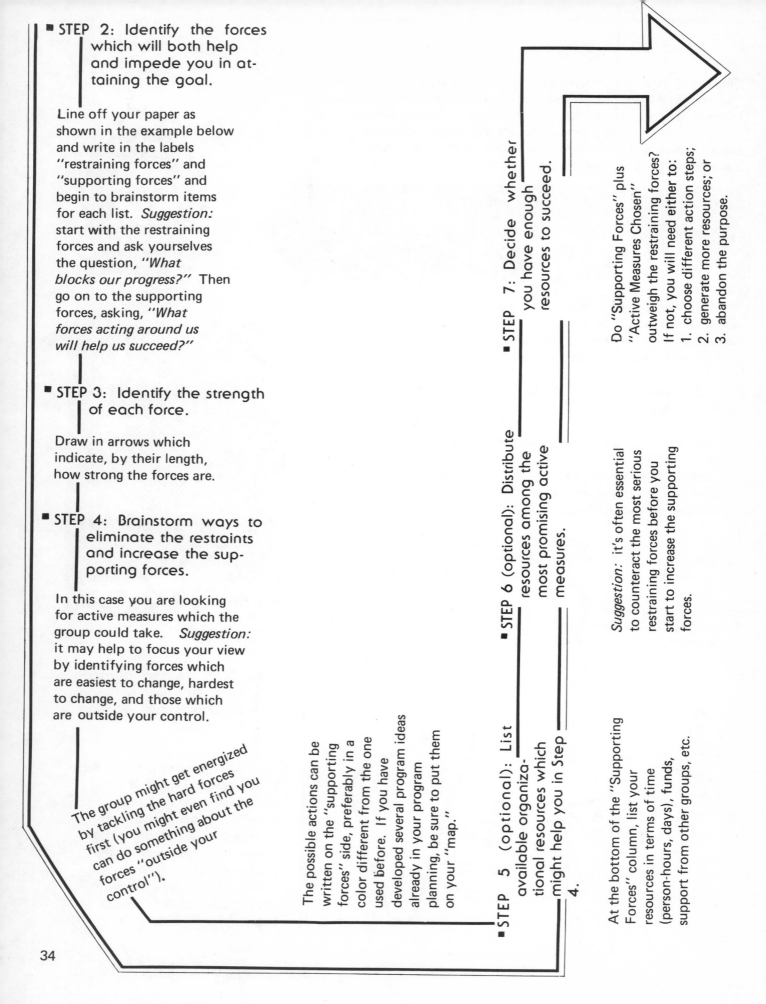

■ STEP 2: Identify the forces
which will both help
and impede you in at-
taining the goal.

Line off your paper as
shown in the example below
and write in the labels
"restraining forces" and
"supporting forces" and
begin to brainstorm items
for each list. *Suggestion:*
start with the restraining
forces and ask yourselves
the question, *"What
blocks our progress?"* Then
go on to the supporting
forces, asking, *"What
forces acting around us
will help us succeed?"*

■ STEP 3: Identify the strength
of each force.

Draw in arrows which
indicate, by their length,
how strong the forces are.

■ STEP 4: Brainstorm ways to
eliminate the restraints
and increase the sup-
porting forces.

In this case you are looking
for active measures which the
group could take. *Suggestion:*
it may help to focus your view
by identifying forces which
are easiest to change, hardest
to change, and those which
are outside your control.

The group might get energized
by tackling the hard forces
first (you might even find you
can do something about the
forces "outside your
control").

The possible actions can be
written on the "supporting
forces" side, preferably in a
color different from the one
used before. If you have
developed several program ideas
already in your program
planning, be sure to put them
on your "map."

■ STEP 5 (optional): List
available organiza-
tional resources which
might help you in Step
4.

At the bottom of the "Supporting
Forces" column, list your
resources in terms of time
(person-hours, days), funds,
support from other groups, etc.

■ STEP 6 (optional): Distribute
resources among the
most promising active
measures.

Suggestion: it's often essential
to counteract the most serious
restraining forces before you
start to increase the supporting
forces.

■ STEP 7: Decide whether
you have enough
resources to succeed.

Do "Supporting Forces" plus
"Active Measures Chosen"
outweigh the restraining forces?
If not, you will need either to:
1. choose different action steps;
2. generate more resources; or
3. abandon the purpose.

Sample Force-Field Analysis

The issue used as an example in the previous section ("**Developing Your Analysis**") is developed here, using the Force-Field technique.

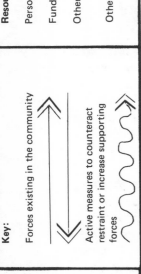

Key:

Forces existing in the community

Active measures to counteract restraint or increase supporting forces

Resources Available:

Person days (PD) - about 50

Funds ($) - about $200 (more possibly)

Other groups' support (OG) - WQQQ - TV
         - Council of Churches

Other resources (R)

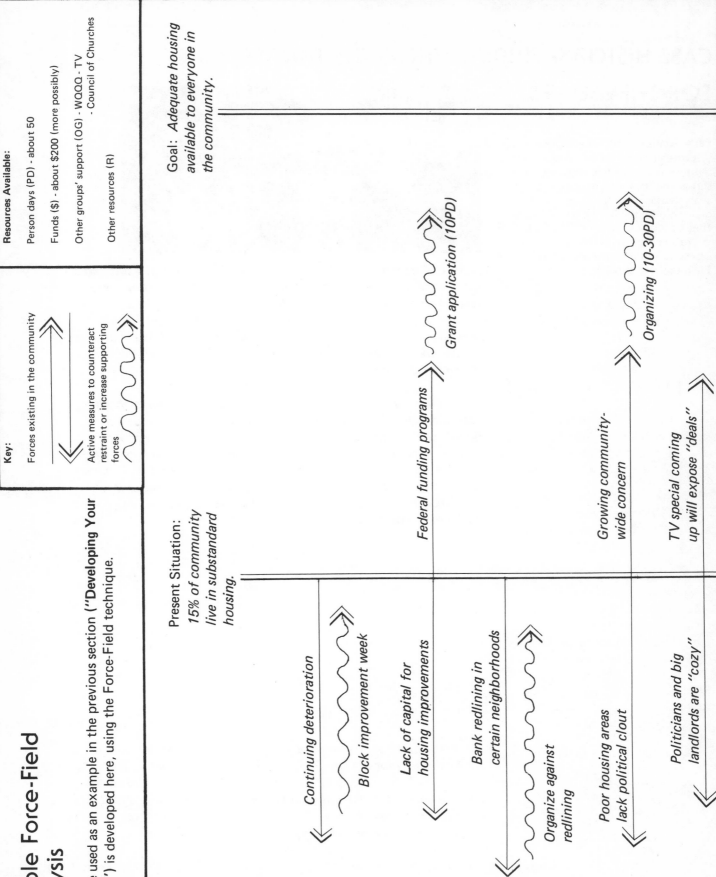

Present Situation:
15% of community live in substandard housing.

Continuing deterioration

Block improvement week

Lack of capital for housing improvements

Bank redlining in certain neighborhoods

Organize against redlining

Poor housing areas lack political clout

Politicians and big landlords are "cozy"

Federal funding programs

Grant application (10PD)

Growing community-wide concern

TV special coming up will expose "deals"

Organizing (10-30PD)

Goal: *Adequate housing available to everyone in the community.*

CASE HISTORY: FINDING THE FACTS THAT SPEAK FOR THEMSELVES

Early attempts at developing an analysis often lead to the conclusion that more facts are needed. A fact-finding survey can provide a basis for further analysis as well as publicity. A Boston organization of working women called **Nine to Five** used a survey to start their campaign for better personnel practices in the publishing industry, as **Ellen Cassedy** explains:

A lot of women came to us from publishing companies and had a number of complaints, including the complaint that they were treated unequally with respect to men—low pay and lack of promotion opportunity. They didn't have any idea about what they wanted to do. The first thing that we decided was that we wanted to make the problem more legitimate by publicizing it, and by doing research.

And so we handed out all these surveys—questionnaires about working conditions and pay and promotion opportunities, and people sent them back in. One thing that did was it managed to contact lots of people—made them aware of our existence. And we became aware of their existence, because they signed their names to these, a lot of them. And then we compiled all of this and we published it in a little booklet, and it looked extremely legitimate and it emboldened people a lot.

Publishing Salaries
in the Boston Area
A Comparison Report

February 1977

✧WOMEN IN PUBLISHING
9 to 5 Organization
140 Clarendon St., Boston 02116

•1.00 members •1.50 nonmembers •5.00 institutions

(With the booklet) we were really armed with some facts, like, for example, that it's worth $3500 a year to be a man—just being a man is worth an extra $3500 a year in publishing! And so that became very concrete and its very specific thing to say, and it was a lot easier, I mean it was a lot stronger than saying, 'I really don't like my job, I just feel that my boss doesn't respect me.'

Duane Dale: *So you're doing several things at the same time—you're gathering facts and you're getting your issue in front of the public, and it sounds like you're developing an analysis of what's going on.*

Cassedy: Right. Then, we held this public forum and we really went all out and recruited for it and not only women in the publishing industry but management came to it, and then we presented all these things, and it was the first time people had ever really seen anybody standing up at a podium saying 'These are problems. These are real problems; it's not just you.'

We got press coverage for it. It really embarassed the companies, put them on the defensive, and that opened the first crack in their defense, because newspapers called them and asked them why they were discriminating. So it really was a good weapon against management.

Meanwhile, one bunch of people are saying we should announce that we're filing suits against the companies. And other people are saying, 'No, let's just get the information out, and give them a chance, and filing a suit is much too strong.'

. . . What ended up happening was one, we got the Attorney General, Belotti, to file suits against the three largest publishing companies in Boston. And then what started happening was the companies started making all kinds of concessions. They were really primed at that point to start increasing salaries for people, particularly the women who were most outspoken, and to change policies.

• How do you personally generate ideas? How does your group best generate ideas?

4

Generating Program Ideas

Some people believe that human beings would generally do nothing if they could—that they are basically lazy, needing strong incentives to get anything accomplished. Others are more optimistic about human nature: people, if adequately fed, sheltered and loved, are very creative, delighting in solving problems and coping with new situations.

Which camp are you closest to and how does that affect your idea of social problems and citizen goals?

Where Do Program Ideas Come From?

There is no sure fire way to generate good program ideas—there are many ways. This section presents several different approaches, each based on a different notion of where program ideas come from.

- Sometimes program ideas come after you have gotten clear on your purposes and then thought carefully about methods to meet a specific purpose.

  If you like that approach, try the activity that has to do with screening and revising possible goal statements, "**Do You Take This Statement to Be Your Lawfully Wedded Goal?**"

- Sometimes the most innovative ideas come from not taking the goal or problem at face value. Citizen groups are in a position to demonstrate innovative approaches to social problems if they can develop their own versions of what's wrong and what can be done about it. If this line of attack intrigues you, try the **"Problem Redefinition"** exercise.

- Sometimes they come from a free-form brainstorm in which participants are welcome to state any idea they have, whether it is a broad purpose or a specific project. If you like this approach, turn to the **"Wish List"** exercise.

- Sometimes they come from bad ideas or from some that just seem "not quite right." One way to turn bland ideas into better ones is found in the activity labeled **"Exploring Options."**

- Sometimes program ideas come from focusing on an examination of the opportunities or resources that a group has available to it. There's also the chance that you will find that the problem you're trying to cope with has a "silver lining"—a possibility for the group to do even *better* than just "setting things right." And so there's an exercise on **"Problem/ Possibility Areas: Opportunity Analysis."**

Do You Take This Statement to Be Your Lawfully Wedded Goal?

Screening Potential Goal Statements

no. people: 3 to many
minimum time: 20 minutes
materials: Copies of the worksheet
on page on pages 42-3.
List of group goals

From time to time in the life of an organization, there develops a
longing for the security and assurance of having a neat and tidy
list of goals. Then, someone, or a committee, will set about to
author a goal statement. It may emerge from a problem statement:
"The goal of this group is to (remedy the problem)." It may emerge
from your analysis of root causes or restraining forces. It may emerge
from your group vision of the ideal situation.

This exercise assumes that you already have drafted a goal statement.
The purpose of the activity is to help your group decide whether it
will accept a particular statement as an official, now-and-ever-after
goal of the group. It will also help participants to learn to distinguish
a goal statement from a nongoal; acquire skills in refining goal statements so that they will be more useful to the group; experience a
process for deciding whether the group will accept a goal.

(Any group that doesn't have a statement of possible goals could
call a quick huddle and come up with one. Don't worry about
the wording—this activity will help you perfect it.)

1. Form groups of three to five people each; if your organization
   is small or your time is abundant, the entire group could work
   together.

2. Distribute one or more "potential goals" to each small group.

3. Designate a facilitator and recorder for each group, who will guide
   the group through the following steps:

   • Write the potential goal statement in its initial form in section A
     of the Goal Revision Worksheet.

   • Discuss the six questions in section B and record the group's
     answers.

   • Draft a "Revised Version #1" of the goal; alternatively, use
     that space on the worksheet to record ideas for improvements,
     suggested rewording of phrases, etc.

   • Draft a "Revised Version #2" and discuss whether it is an
     acceptable statement of the goal. The group may wish to
     answer the six questions again with respect to the revised
     version.

Goal Revision worksheet

Initial Goal Statement

	Questions			Comments
1	*Is the statement a statement of future intention—an event or situation that would take place in the future?*	yes ☐	no ☐	If not, it's probably not a goal; try to rewrite so the answer will be "yes."
2	*Is the statement made in terms of the outside world, or in terms of what the group will do?*	yes ☐	no ☐	A statement in terms of what the group will do is probably a strategy for achieving some goal. Ask yourselves, "What do we want this group activity to accomplish?"
3	*Is that statement clear enough that you will be able to tell when you have reached the goal?*	yes ☐	no ☐	The most useful goal statements are those with criteria built into them: "All Senior Citizens in town will have access to hot lunches." The goal statement needs to describe an observable situation or event.
4	*Is the goal feasible for the group to achieve?*	yes ☐	no ☐	There's nothing wrong with ambitious ambitious goals, but at least some should be well enough within reach that the group can sense the prospect of success. Rewrite if you need to.
5	*Does the goal fall within the mandate or broad purpose which brought the group together in the first place?*	yes ☐	no ☐	A small group will have to bring this question to the organization as a whole to find out for sure, though it might offer the opinion that a particular goal is not within the organization's "ball park."
6	*Is the group really committed to the goal?*	yes ☐	no ☐	No use having a batch of goals that sit on the shelf gathering dust. Unless the organization is really willing to "get married to" a goal and work with it, you'd be better off to scratch it off the list. Better to have a short list of "live" goals which will really be used as a basis for selecting programs, as inspiration, as a reminder of what the organization is all about!

Revised Version #1

Revised Version #2

After you're satisfied with the wording of the goal, share your work with the other small groups. Here are some additional questions which you may want to consider:

Discussion Questions

- *Does the combined list of goals reflect the full range of concerns on which your group is based?*

- *Is the combined list short enough to be manageable? Keep in mind that the objectives of specific projects can be spelled out later.*

- *Do the goals generate excitement? Do they clarify the reason that the group has joined together?*

- *If any of the answers were "no," what do you need to reword or change?*

Once you're satisfied with your list of goals, you may want to take it with you to the next activity -- **"Wish List"** -- which suggests ways of generating specific project ideas.

Creating a Vision: Wish List

no. people: 3 to many ⊦
minimum time: 15 minutes
materials: newsprint, felt pens

Now is the time to recruit as many people as possible for some creative thinking. The purpose of this activity is to generate as many as possible about programs/activities for your group.

1. Invite group members, staff and even the community at large to a "Where do we go from here?" meeting. Write one of the following questions on newsprint or on a large sheet of paper and hang it on the wall:

   • *What* should *our group be doing?*

   • *In the best of all worlds, with unlimited resources, what could our group do over the next few years?*

   • *What are some project ideas that might help us carry out our purposes?*

2. Start brainstorming ideas (see box for guidelines). Spend no more than fifteen minutes on this; the point is to get a lot of ideas out, fast.

3. It may help to refer to goal statements, analysis statements, force-field diagrams, old idea lists, etc.

Guidelines for Brainstorming

Brainstorming is one method which can help a group of people get involved together in the process of generating creative ideas. A facilitator writes the topic or question to be brainstormed at the top of a large sheet of paper, then asks the group to call out their ideas in short phrases which can be written down quickly. In order to set a creative, high-energy tone, the following guidelines should be stated to the group from the onset:

• No judgements. No idea or suggestion, no matter how wild, is to be shot down, or edited. (There'll be time to evaluate the ideas later.)

• Anything goes. Offbeat, unusual, humorous and bizarre ideas are encouraged.

• Go for *quantity*. The more ideas, the better the chance of coming up with a winner.

• Building on other people's ideas is fine.

The facilitator of the brainstorm can help to keep things moving, if necessary, by 1. Setting a time limit—commonly 3 to 10 minutes (depending on topic and size of group), so that people will know they can't afford to sit on an idea; 2. giving a few examples to start things off (a "hailstorm"); 3. praising, coaxing (gently); 4. asking for different *sorts* of examples if the group starts to develop a "one track mind."

The conventional approach is to have one person record the group's ideas on newsprint with a felt marker, so that all can see. Sometimes two recorders work as a team, writing alternate items, so that the group won't have to wait for the recorders to catch up.

Another variation that is especially useful if you have several topics to brainstorm is to write each topic on a separate sheet of newsprint paper, and provide each participant with a marker so they can go up to the lists and record items "grafitti-style."

Recent research indicates that brainstorming is *not necessarily* the best technique to generate lots of creative ideas. The problem seems to be that a group of people can go off on one tangent without exploring the full range of possibilities. This suggests several **variations** of the brainstorming process:

Variation 1: Instruct each group member to brainstorm *individually* on the topic, writing down ideas on a small piece of paper. Then share the ideas by reading off the lists (or compiling the lists later).

Variation 2: Divide the group into two or more teams, each to brainstorm on the same topic. This "parallel groups" approach has some of the advantage of Variation 1, plus the sense of group cooperation which is an important side-effect of brainstorming.

Despite its limitations, brainstorming remains a popular technique. For many groups, it has provided a first clear picture of their potential to think creatively together and to move off in new directions. It also lets everyone know where the ideas have come from, thus setting the stage for consensus and action.

You may want to keep the list posted for several weeks or months to provide a chance for late additions. You will probably find that a number of your brainstormed ideas are actually programs that have been run by other organizations. This is probably the most common source of program ideas, and you may want to develop more ways to learn about other groups' projects. Common sources of information are newsletters (try for a subscription exchange), conferences, support groups, phone calls, and the mass media.

4. Toward the end of a brainstorm, the facilitator can provide a little prompting: "Have you heard of other groups doing projects that we might want to try?"

   For the long run, the question is whether your group wants to maintain closer touch with other groups tackling the same issues, and if so, *who will do it and how?*

5. Once you have a long and varied list of project possibilities, Section 5 of this manual, "Choosing a Program," will help you narrow your choices and select the best.

   First, however, there are some additional methods for generating project ideas and developing them.

CASE HISTORY: BRAINSTORMING UNDER PRESSURE

Brainstorming isn't always done in the quietude of a planning meeting. Sometimes it occurs in the crowded, chaotic situations which may emerge during a protest demonstration or some other type of citizen action. **Frances Crowe**, a dedicated social activist and trainer from Northampton, Massachusetts, explained to us how she wound up using brainstorming with a group of college women who were staging a demonstration at the University of Massachusetts to secure more and better coverage of women's issues in the student newspaper, the **Daily Collegian**.

*I had heard that they had a demonstration going last Monday, and it didn't sound too good to me. They had taken the **Collegians** and put them in a pile on the floor and then they started walking around them and chanting, and people were trying to break through the line and grab their **Collegians**. They were pinching the women; they were going up in the balcony and throwing stuff down on them, so it got to be quite an ugly scene.*

Tuesday morning early somebody called me and said "We think we need some help with this" And so I said I'd be right over.

*We sat down and brainstormed how we might raise the issue of needing women's pages in the **Collegian** without actually causing so much disruption. We came up with the idea that maybe there was no way we were going to be able to really stop people from taking the **Collegians**, that maybe what we should do is get a couple of boxes and magic markers and get people to take their **Collegians** and say "Would you, when you're finished with your **Collegian**, would you mark on the front of it 'I support four pages of women's news once a week in the **Collegian**.' And then when you're ready to throw it away, dispose of it in this box, and we'll deliver it to the **Collegian**."*

*And things went much better. I think that the women who were running it felt very positive about that, and we got a lot of **Collegians** Collected. We had to run around fast, you know, to make signs and be there, but it helped them feel that there was a whole other way, and that with a little bit of pre-planning, it could go better.*

Playing with a Full Deck: Exploring Options

no. people: one to 20
minimum time: 20 minutes
materials: newsprint and felt pens

Here's a way to start with a program idea that isn't quite right and develop a better one. Actually it's a good approach any time you seem to be moving too quickly to a choice without exploring other options. It can be done by an individual or by a group of as many as 20 or so.

Some experts say that programs should be planned by *starting* with goal statements, but not everyone thinks in such a neat, rational sequence. This activity is handy if you have started with a program idea or two and you sense a need to think about *why* you might want to do them and *what* some other options would be. The official sequence is *Goals—Program Ideas—Detailed Plans.* The *why* and *what* questions lead to this sequence: *Original Program Idea—Why?—Goals—What?—Other Program Ideas—Choice—Detailed Plans.*

1. Write the program idea(s) on newsprint. Draw a line, and write the word "Why?"

2. Go around the group, asking participants *why* the group might undertake the proposed activity. Variations on this question could be asked instead: "If we did this, what would we get out of it? What purpose would it serve? What would we hope to achieve?" Sometimes it's useful to push the questioning even further: "Why would we want to do *that*?" could be asked of the replies. The objective is to get back to the real purpose of the activity.

3. Once enough people have had their say, it makes sense to summarize the purpose in a sentence or two. The assumption of this activity is that if the idea seemed interesting at all it was because its purpose had some appeal. And if we can state that purpose—make it explicit—then we're ready to ask the second question: "What else could we do that might serve that purpose?"
   You're in a position to use a brainstorm approach (see the Wish List exercise) to try to get some fresh answers.

Problem Redefinition

Too many people spend their lives trying to solve the *wrong* problem. For example: Long, long ago, as the story goes, a company that had been selling walnuts in the shell decided that it wanted to be the first company to offer shelled, whole walnuts. The company executives gathered a team of its best and its brightest, and they all thought very hard about how to break into a walnut shell without scrunching the walnut meat inside. One day, they were about to conclude that the problem had no solution at all, but as the team of inventive people stood in the company cafeteria line discussing the problem, the cook—who had overheard them—offered this clue:

"Well, you know, there are lots of different ways to crack an egg: you can crack 'em with a knife, you can crack 'em on the edge of the bowl, you can even crack one egg with another egg. But the feller who does the neatest job cracking eggs is the chick who's trying to get out."

"Aha!" said one of the best and brightest, "All this time we've been trying to crack into the walnut from the outside. If only there was a way to crack a walnut from the *inside*!"

(The solution they came up with was to stick a hypodermic needle into each walnut and puff it up with air until the shell exploded away!) **The moral of the story is that you're not likely to get a new solution if you keep looking at the problem in the same old way.**

NEW SOLUTIONS DEMAND... NEW WAYS OF SEEING

Does this apply to citizen groups? We think so. Often, there's an established way of doing things. A school assumes that a student who's doing poorly needs more time with the teacher or the textbooks; a job training program assumes that an unemployed person may need to acquire more job skills; a neighborhood group assumes that an apathetic group needs a block party to increase community-mindedness. Each of these groups may be treating the wrong problem, and if so, they're wasting time and money doing it.

Any citizen group that wants to make sure its program idea is worth the bother might think about probing for *alternative definitions* of the problem it's trying to solve. There's more than one way to redefine a problem; if the first doesn't work, try harder.

Method 1: The Gap

You'll need three sheets of newsprint, felt-tipped pens, and a general idea of the problem area or goal. Label one newsprint sheet, *"The Ideal"*; the second, *"The Real"*; and the third is *"The Gap."* The group should list aspects of the ideal (situations or events, as specifically as possible), and do the same for the real (the present situation). Then the two sheets should be compared and the differences recorded under the heading, *"The Gap."* According to one definition, a problem is "the difference between ideal and actual"—and so the *gap* should, by definition, be the problem. You should ask yourselves whether it really is—and you will probably want to summarize the *gap* items into a problem statement.

Method 2: Whose View?

The "secret" of this method is that a problem may look different to different people.

1. Ask yourself in whose view your problem is now stated.

2. Take on some other views, by imagining yourself as the person who has the problem, your grandmother, your granddaughter, the secretary general of the U.N., an undernourished person in a less developed country, and so on.

3. Imagine yourself to be each of these people or, if at all possible, go and ask them what they think the real problem is. Then summarize your findings.

Problem/Possibility Areas: Opportunity Analysis

no. people: one to many
minimum time: 20 minutes
materials: pen and paper or newsprint and
felt pens.

There is a tendency in our society to create programs by starting with
a *problem* statement. This is often useful, but it overlooks the
possibility that we might want ot go further than just "ironing out
the wrinkles" in the social fabric—we might want to make things
much better, rather than just to "solve problems."

Futurist Robert Theobald takes this into account when he talks
about "Problem/Possibility Areas." Every problem implies
some possibilities or opportunities. Let's not settle for curing
the patient—the objective should be to help the person become
a vibrantly healthy human being. And sometimes, if we look
only for "problems" to solve, we miss the golden opportunities
that are right in front of us.

1. List all the group's opportunities that you can think of. The
   following categories may help suggest opportunities to you:
   • abilities and interests of group members
   • untapped community resources—for example, people with
     knowledge, contacts, money, or time
   • utopian visions and practical ideas for a better community.

2. Review any problem lists you have (from previous activities), or
   write a brief problem statement. Then look for the "other side
   of the coin"—the positive outcomes that might be achieved.

3. Push a little harder: imagine that your group is very successful;
   what positive changes could it bring about?

4. Your list at this point may be a hodgepodge of program ideas,
   people-resources, interests, and so on. See which can be turned
   into program ideas. Then take your list to the "Choosing a
   Program" section, with a stopover, if you like, at the following
   paragraphs on developing a program idea.

CASE HISTORY: SOMETHING BORROWED

Sometimes the best program ideas for a particular situation are ones which other groups have already tried and found effective. Here's an example from the Boston women's organization, **Nine to Five.**

Ellen Cassedy: *There was the* Petty Office Procedures Contest. *that we did last year, where we asked people to send in their entry for the most ridiculous thing they'd been asked to do in an office, and we awarded the prize to a boss who asked his secretary to sew up a rip in his pants while he was still wearing them.*

Duane Dale: *How did you ever come up with that?*

Cassedy: *Actually, we got the idea from another working women's organization, and I don't know how they thought it up.*

Dale: *Did one particular person hear about this idea from the other organization, or . . .*

Cassedy: *I think they probably read about it in a newsletter from one of the other organizations, and the Executive Board* [**of Nine to Five**] *, which is about ten people, was fishing around for something to do toward the end of the summer that would be a good filler kind of thing to do, and decided that this would be good. A lot of what we do takes a year, and it's hard to follow if you're not involved in the organization, so what we wanted was something that would catch the imagination of people who were not involved day-to-day, that would reach out so that people could understand it instantly and just get a charge out of it right away.*

. . . It was an example of something that was successful—it was short, it didn't try to do a tremendous amount, and it didn't take very much energy. But it got a lot of press, and it got people involved.

Developing a Program Idea

Program ideas often appear as mere nuggets or kernels: "run a community health fair," or "start an oral history project." The next step is to develop the kernels into full-blown program ideas. This will serve two purposes: 1. everyone will have approximately the same notion of what is being considered, and 2. you will begin to anticipate problems or think of the little improvements which could assure success. The point is to take an abstract idea and *make it real* in people's minds—before it happens, even before the group has to choose one alternative future for itself over another.

Here are some ways you can do this, either as an individual, a planning committee, or in small teams within a planning workshop:

• Draw sketches or build a model.

Several years ago, the University of Massachusetts was planning its first "Toward Tomorrow Fair" —a festival of alternatives in energy, housing, social action, and lifestyle. A simple aerial sketch of the fairgrounds went a long way in explaining to interested parties (including funding sources) what was planned. The sketch also drew attention to the importance of colorful banners and pendants to add eye-appeal to the fairgrounds.

One doesn't need to be a polished artist to draw sketches that will serve the purpose. For certain sorts of projects a three-dimensional model, made from inexpensive or recycled materials, may be even more useful.

• Develop a rough schedule of events.

Whether you're talking about a one-night discussion program or a year-long petition drive and organizing campaign, a step-by-step list of events will flesh out the concept and identify possible snags and alternatives.

• Write a script.

This carries the previous idea a bit further. If your proposed program involves talking with someone—neighbors by telephone, officials at City Hall, or people who stop at a booth— write a script of the probable conversation. In some cases, this is exactly the sort of information that will make your idea "more real" to other group members and allow allow them to decide whether to "buy in."

- Develop a rough implementation plan.

Take a systematic approach: fill out the planning list below, giving your best guess about each item.

Number (and names) of people involved:
Starting and ending dates:
Average number of hours/person:
Types of tasks involved:
Costs:
Milestones:
How we'll know when we've succeeded:

Contingency Planning

no. people: 5 or more
minimum time: 15 minutes
materials: newsprint, felt pens

Contingency planning can be used to anticipate problems and plan for them *before* they happen. It can also be used to build flexibility into the plan by identifying choice points at which alternate plans can be introduced.

This activity can be used to develop a program idea you have been considering, or you may want to try out the contingency planning process using this hypothetical situation:

> Suppose that your group has decided to raise funds by throwing a spectacular party; you want to be sure that it comes off smoothly.

1. Form groups of at least five people each; larger groups will produce faster-moving brainstorms, but smaller groups will encourage more individual participation in discussion.

2. Identify a facilitator-recorder in each group, who will lead a brainstorm on events which could disrupt the plan. (See Brainstorm Guidelines, pages 44-5 .)

3. Put the topic for the brainstorm at the top of a newsprint sheet, (such as): Events which could disrupt the *spectacular fund-raising party.* Spend five or ten minutes brainstorming possible disruptive events.

4. After you have a list of possible disruptions, choose a few of them and decide how you might respond to each. For example, if you wanted to prepare for hail during an outdoor party, you might want to be ready to move inside or build a geodesic dome over the party, or provide table-tennis paddles to bat the hailstones away.

5. If there is time, use a similar process to identify points where the flexibility of alternative plans would be desirable. Have the group review the program plan and identify the choice points; list these on newsprint. Then, beside each choice point, list possible alternative plans.

Discussion

Using contingency planning requires decisions as to *which* fallback plans are worth developing, and this calls for the same sort of consensus building and decision-making as the main plan. The cost of preparing a backup plan will need to be weighed against the benefits that result and the likelihood that the fallback plan will actually be needed. In a real situation, it would be important to help the group decide which options it wanted to pursue. Workshop participants may want to share opinions about the usefulness of the process; they may come up with variations that would fit their particular situation.

- How do you decide whether there is enough support for a particular idea to choose it? Does the majority rule? Two-thirds vote? Consensus? Is there a way to incorporate the minority view?

- How do you decide when it's time to stop generating new program ideas and start choosing?

5

Choosing a Program

So far, we assume, you've been exploring several—maybe many—alternative program ideas, keeping an open mind, pausing to consider some paths that won't be taken. Eventually, the time comes to decide what your organization will and won't do.

There are several key aspects to this decision, and they can be summarized as questions:

- *Do we* want *to do it?*

- *How well does a program fulfill our goals?*

- *How important is the outcome in the eyes of the members? Does it have any negative impacts?*

- *Can* we *do it?*

- *Is it feasible, given the money, time, skills, and other resources that we have?*

- *Does it allow enough time for other important activities?*

- *Are there forces operating outside (or within) the group that will prevent its success?*

Once these two groups of questions are considered and facts, opinions, and forecasts are gathered, it becomes possible to ask:

- *Which of our program ideas do we* most want *to implement?*

- *Do we have a strong enough commitment as an organization and as individuals to make the **project** succeed?*

Activities in this section provide ways to deal with these questions.

How Closely Does Each Program Idea Relate to Your Goals?

no. people: 1
minimum time: 5 min.
materials: form below

This is an opportunity for you to dust off your goal statement(s) and put it to good use. One criterion for choosing a program from a pool of ideas is to determine how closely it "matches" your group's purpose and goals.

1. With your goal statement in hand, indicate in the space below how closely each program idea will help fulfill the organization's goals. Each idea should be rated on a scale of 1 to 10 (1=poor match; 10=excellent match). If more than one person participates in this activity, total the individual scores.

Program Idea	Individual Ratings (1-10)	Group Totals
Idea Number 1		
Idea Number 2		
Idea Number 3		
Idea Number 4		
Idea Number 5		

2. You may want to take the ideas with the highest scores and test the desirability and feasibility of each idea. (See the next exercise.)

CASE HISTORY: A COMMUNITY CANNING CENTER

Each exercise so far is one step in an overall planning process; in a real case the steps have to fit together and build into a program. One project which did particularly well at developing an analysis, exploring alternatives, and also testing desirability was the self-help Community Canning Center Project, started by **Women in Agriculture**. To learn about it, we interviewed **Pat Sackrey**, one of the original members of the group.

Sackrey: *In 1975 I was involved in developing the first self-help canning center in Massachusetts, which exists at 33 King Street in Northampton. It grew out of our study group [which was] involved in the politics of agriculture and land use and food policy. We wanted to know what on earth we could do as a little group to help revitalize agriculture in Massachusetts and New England generally, so we could become more self-reliant. You know, importing 85% of our food was, we thought, making us terribly vulnerable as a people, and it was a very poor use of our land and human, natural resources too. So we did a lot of thinking and studying and talking and reading and meeting together as a very small group of women and men to look primarily at where the gaps were.*

Analysis: restraining forces *And there were a lot of them: The whole support structure for the agricultural endeavors of our state had declined enormously; for example, there were no processing plants for food that was grown here. We have a short growing season, but there was no warehousing for grains and root vegetables. There was also the problem of supplies. When you have a diminishing number of farmers the businesses that take care of agriculture can't support themselves. And it looked like in some areas we had reached the critical limit, and maybe gone below it.*

Goal-setting

Alternative program ideas *One problem had to do with the gap between growers in Massachusetts and consumers in Massachusetts. It seemed to us that they weren't getting together very well. Growers were growing things in the fields; a lot of them were turning over surplus crops at the end of the year, not getting good sales for what they were growing. And the consumers were buying their food from the major grocery chains, who weren't buying local produce. So we looked into why that was and we understood some of the reasons, and we thought 'Well, maybe we could start just in a little way solving that problem by providing a way that people could preserve food." And there were a lot of choices we could have made—a small commercial cannery, a community freezer, working very hard only on the supermarkets, demanding that they buy local produce, working on legislation that would require certain kinds of businesses in Massachusetts to buy from local businesses—there were a lot of ways we could have gone.*

There were two reasons we went [the route of a] self-help canning center. One was that we learned about the technology which was available. Ball Canning Company had come out with a community canning system—small, easy to work, safe, didn't take too much room. And the second thing was there was money available through the Governor's office—a special CETA manpower grant for local initiative projects.

So we decided that we would go that way, because it was clear—the path was clear. We knew it was going to be a lot of work, but we thought we had the people that could write the proposals and do the politicking—it was a very political process, as all these things are.

And so we did it. And it went well, it's gone well since, it's grown, and this year there are five canning centers starting in Massachusetts, based on ours. That was our idea you know, to try in just a little way to solve a big problem at the local level in such a way that other people could copy it if they thought it was a good idea.

Duane Dale: *What strikes me is that you apparently entered into the thing not knowing what your program would do and yet you were prepared to spend some time together as a study group.*

Sackrey: *Yeah, well we just knew that we were all interested in this problem of agriculture and food, and we were called* **Women In Agriculture** *just because of my being on the* **Commission on the Status of Women,** *and my saying in the paper that I wanted to work on women in agriculture, and other people calling and saying "I want to work on that too."*

Dale: *How many people were in the study group?*

Sackrey: *Seven.*

Dale: *How long was it from when you first started to meet until you started to really consider the canning center project?*

Sackrey: *About seven months. It was about four or five months until we started saying, "We've got to do something about this gap between growers and consumers. That's something we can address."*

We agreed from the beginning that we wanted to be an action-oriented group, not just a study group. But we also agreed we had to know more than we did.

Dale: *So it was four or five months of just exploring the problem . . . .*

Sackrey: *Yes, and meeting together, in very loose ways, you know, we just really deliberately stayed small so we could just be informal and not have to "administer" ourselves. I for one was tired of being an administrator for a while.*

Dale:	*How often did you meet?*
Sackrey:	*We met every week.*
Dale:	*A couple of hours?*
Sackrey:	*More, usually.*
Dale:	*And how long did you keep meeting?*
Sackrey:	*Oh, we're still going. We're now working on a project—see, we got jobs for some of the members of the group at the canning center. Now we've got a job for one of our members coordinating the planning and implementation of our largest project to date, which is the New England Small Farm Institute.*

Desirability: Pros and Cons

no. people: 3 to many!
minimum time: 15 minutes
materials: form below, newsprint and felt pen

If you're considering several program ideas, you'll need a way to
compare their advantages and disadvantages. (If you have more
than three or four ideas, you'll probably want to boil them down
to three. You can do this in a workshop situation by giving
every group member three votes and keeping the ideas that
receive the most votes. You may need to allow some discussion
and lobbying time before your vote.)

1. Using a felt-tipped pen and a large sheet of newsprint, layout the following grid:

Program Idea: write a brief name or description	Plus	Minus
• Idea Number 1		
• Idea Number 2		
• Idea Number 3		

2. As a group, consider each idea and call out benefits and problems,
   which someone will record. For example, a member might say,
   "A *plus* is that it will take a short time to do the project," or
   " A *minus* is that it will cost us $300." It may be desirable to
   give some "clues" to the group as it lists items. You could write
   these phrases on the newsprint, perhaps in a different color:
   plus—fulfills goals, builds community support, and so on; *minus*
   —costs, time, "side effects," and so on.

3. Stand back and look at what you have. Decide whether there is
   enough information for comparison of the program ideas. If so,
   move on to your decision; if not, think about what additional
   information you need.

Is It Feasible?
Resources: Needed and Available

"You can't do everything you want to do."

It's as true in a citizen group as it is at the amusement park: riding the bumper cars all day is just too expensive. So the problem is to compare the resources that are needed for a particular project with the resources available and likely. This form could help you do that.

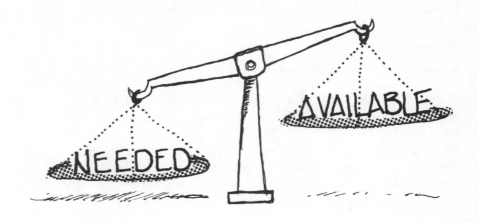

Program Idea:					
Resource	**Amount Needed** Real	Ideal		**Amount Available** On Hand	Likely
Time (overall, in person-hours)					
Time for particular key individuals: (name) (name) (name) (name)					
Dollar cost					
Cooperation of other organizations					
Community support					
Physical space					
Other					

Note: In order to complete the top three sections of the chart, you may want to make up a rough timeline (or task list) and a rough budget. The remaining items aren't as easy to measure; you will need to think about requirements and availability, and specify them as best you can. And of course it's important to think carefully about the additional (unique) resources that your program idea may require.

"Zap Analysis;" or, Don't Let It Rain on My Parade

no. people: one to several
minimum time: 10 minutes
materials: form below

"Zap Analysis" is our own phrase for analyzing the things that could pop up and upset your program—the "zaps". This is part of examining the feasibility of the project because you may not want to start a project that's very susceptible to zaps. It's also the first step in contingency planning (see page   ) but here the purpose is to consider whether a plan is so "zap-able" that a less risky plan should be chosen instead.

1. Identify the **program** idea that you are zap-analyzing. Write it down, so that everyone knows just what you're talking about.

2. List potential zaps in the left-hand column of the form below. Challenge yourselves to be very imaginative. Play the part of Mephistopheles himself, bent on throwing a monkey-wrench in the works.

3. Think harder. Would any of these affect your program: bad weather, the World Series, someone's death, the church Strawberry Supper, the president's death, a telephone company strike, a power failure, leap year? What if the grocery store is out of napkins, the plumber can't come 'til Monday, you forgot the extension cord? Also, think about each resource that's crucial for your success, and ask yourself what that depends on.

4. Now fill out the other columns for each item on the list, as a way of deciding how worrisome the potential zap is.

Discussion Questions

- *What assumptions about people does the potential program make?*

- *What are the implications of each "zap" and what can be done if the zap occurs no matter how well you plan?*

Program Idea:			
Potential Zap	*How Likely? (%)*	*How Disruptive?*	*Possible to Plan Around It?*
•	•	•	•
•	•	•	•
•	•	•	•

- How can your group set a timeline and stick to it?

- What can be done to make sure that people's skills are being fully utilized?

- What sort of help and "moral support" do people need in order to get their job done?

- Who are potential supporters of your project?

6 Strategies: Making Programs Happen

This section has to do with planning to carry out your chosen program idea. It has to do with the nitty-gritty of task assignments, timelines and deadlines, gathering resources, and building community support. The **Citizen Involvement Training Project** will be publishing manuals on organizing, organizational development, and using the media, which may also be useful at this point.

Lining Up Support

no. people: one to several
minimum time: 20 minutes
materials: form below

Any well-intended project can flop if it doesn't have support. The tricky part is trying to figure out how to build the support you need.

1. Each person should fill out the chart below, identifying individuals who fall into one of three categories (15 min.).

2. With a plus (+), indicate which of those in the second column could be enlisted with minimal effort. With an x, indicate the people in the second and third columns who are crucial—those who need to support your project in order for it to succeed. Put an asterisk (*) next to people whom you know well and would be willing to contact.

People/groups who support our project *	People/groups who are neutral about the project + x *	People/groups who are against the project x *

Discussion Questions

- *Is there agreement about who needs to be persuaded?*

- *Who will be important but difficult to persuade?*

- *What are the ways you could go about eliciting their support? (Try brainstorming tactics).*

- *Who will be responsible for lining up support from specific groups or individuals? See next exercise for ideas about clarifying responsibilities and deadlines.*

Who Should Do What By When?

no. people: 3 to several
minimum time: 45 min.
materials: newsprint, felt pens, small slips
           of paper

Once your group has selected a specific program, you'll need a method of allocating responsibilities and making sure that everything gets done on time. Sometimes there is confusion about who's responsible for what, or a deadline may "slide by" and things get behind schedule.

One way to limit the role confusion and enforce deadlines is to involve workers early in the planning process. This does two things: first, everyone has an equal say in how responsibilities are allocated and has a sense of the program as a whole; and second, if tasks don't get done, peer pressure can and probably will be exerted on "the offender."

1. Call a meeting of everyone who will be or could be working on the program, including staff members, committee members, volunteers, and so on (this is a good time to recruit volunteers for specific tasks).

2. Have a quick brainstorming session to get a list of all the activities/tasks that need to be done to implement the program.

3. Taking one task at a time, ask for suggestions about deadlines and responsibility. Once all suggestions are on the floor, go over each, asking for a rationale. If there is confusion and/or disagreement, ask each person to explain her concerns in depth. This process of "checking out" areas of disagreement usually leads to acceptance and/or compromises. (The amount of time to allot to this task will vary, depending on the number of people in the group and the complexity of the task.)

Here's another simple, straightforward approach to timelining that can be used by one person or a team. It is an adaption of the PERT approach (Program Evaluation and Review Technique), which has recently become popular in government and business planning.

no. people: 3 to many
minimum time: 45 minutes
materials: shelf or roll paper, small slips of
           paper.

1. Brainstorm the tasks involved in your project. Be as thorough as possible; the level of detail you choose will depend on the complexity of your project—but probably 100 tasks would be the maximum you could feasibly handle (without a computer). *Don't write the tasks on one sheet of paper; write one each on small slips of paper*—say, 2 x 3 inches; if a group is doing the exercise, use larger slips and larger printing.

2. Stretch out some shelf paper (or other roll-paper) on a tabletop or on the floor. Mark off weeks or months along the length of the paper, allowing enough space to spread your task slips out along the paper.

3. Put the task slips down, and start grouping them by type: publicity tasks go together, fund-raising tasks go together, and so on. You will have to decide what categories or "tracks" will produce the neatest results.

4. Now take each group of slips and arrange the tasks in the appropriate sequence. Estimate how long each task will take to complete and write that time in the bottom right corner, then position each slip on the time grid. Do the same for all the groups of slips. The easiest procedure is often to start with the last task and work back from there. Add more task slips as you think of them.

5. Think about how one "track" relates to another. The objective is to come up with a time-line that looks like a railroad switching yard. Every time one track needs the information or other product of another track, connect them with arrows.

Sample Timeline: Task/Who/When Format

Project: Fund-Raising Party

Task	Who	When
Send invitation	Sue	Oct. 5
Order food	Sam	Oct. 25
Greet guests	Sally & Seldon	Oct 31; 8-9 p.m.
Clean-up	All	Nov. 1; 9 a.m. until done

Advantages: easy to understand; clarifies responsibilities and deadlines.

Drawbacks: Doesn't show how tasks are related to each other.

Sample Timeline: PERT Format

Project: Publicize Community Meeting

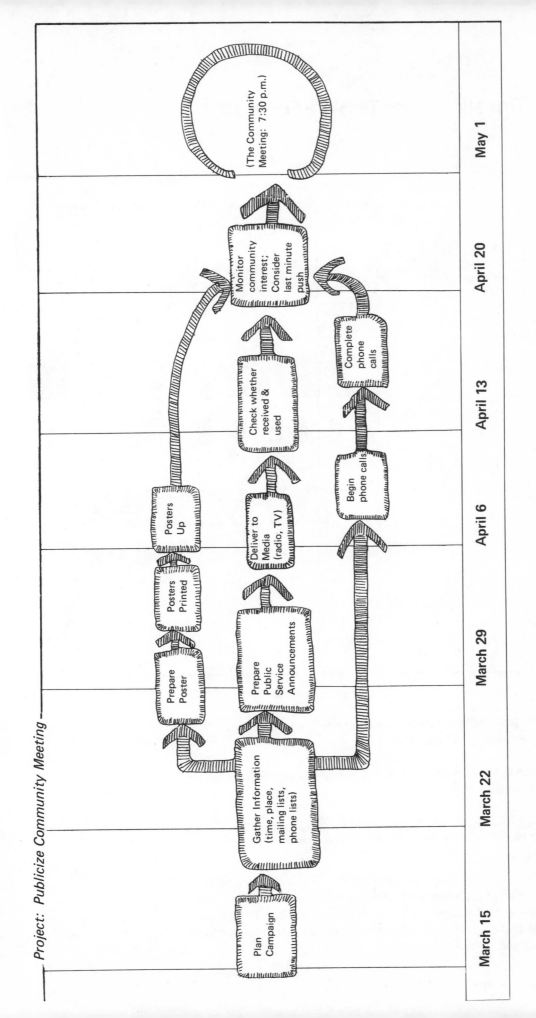

March 15	March 22	March 29	April 6	April 13	April 20	May 1

Advantages: Shows sequence of tasks; shows what tasks will be simultaneous.

Disadvantages: Takes time to understand; doesn't clarify responsibilities (unless initials are added in boxes).

69

Sample Timeline: Bar Graph Format

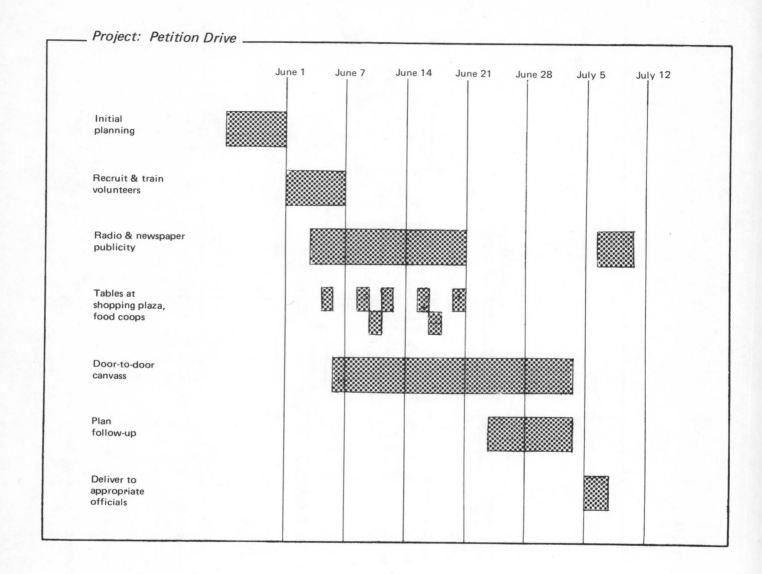

Project: Petition Drive

	June 1	June 7	June 14	June 21	June 28	July 5	July 12

Initial planning

Recruit & train volunteers

Radio & newspaper publicity

Tables at shopping plaza, food coops

Door-to-door canvass

Plan follow-up

Deliver to appropriate officials

Advantages: Shows relationship between activities; clear overview of all activities.

Disadvantages: Doesn't show individual responsibilities; doesn't show specific tasks.

Note: For complex projects, a Bar Graph or PERT format can provide an overview, and Task/Who/When charts can provide detail for each component.

6. Stand back and look at what you've created. Think about whether it adequately shows the tasks involved, the sequence of events, a realistic estimate of the time required (considering both the person-hours needed and also the inevitable time lags), and the connections between tasks and "tracks."

7. You can treat the timeline you've created as a draft and polish it using the following procedures:

Rewrite tasks as events: "Start calls to town fathers (and mothers)"; "Complete calls to local officials." "Start" and "Complete" on the same task can be connected with an arrow or string, showing the duration of that task. Be sure the wording describes clear, "do-able" job is done ("Calls completed to 25 businesspeople").

See that each portion of the timeline (PERT chart) has about the same level of detail. It may be desirable for the workers on each "track" to plan their activities in greater detail, but they can do that separately.

Discussion Questions

- *Which track is the most crucial in terms of deciding whether the project can be completed on schedule?* This is the track which must be monitored most closely, with extra help available if necessary to keep it on schedule.

- *Which tasks can be done early and gotten out of the way?*

- *Which tasks can be done at any point in the sequence because they are relatively independent of other tasks?*

Support Systems: Getting What you Need

Even an organization that plans well may fall down if it doesn't have the sort of support system people need to get their tasks accomplished. So let's look at what you need by way of support:

Support System Questionnaire

(To be answered alone, in pairs, or in small groups.)

1. Think of times you have been very productive. What was your task or project?

2. Who were the other people on the scene? What sort of support, encouragement, or expectations did they contribute?

3. What does that tell you about the help that others can provide to you?

4. What could you do to create a similar support system for yourself now? How could this group (present organization) help?

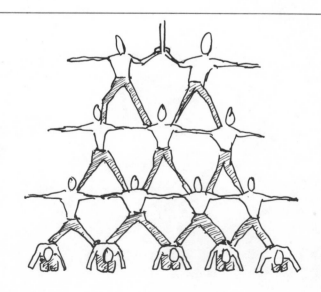

Whether your organization has committees, task forces, or support groups as its structure, the idea is the same: you're gathering together with other people who (hopefully) share a commitment to a purpose, and also an interest in each other as human beings. You meet together primarily to exchange ideas and to get a job done. To do that most effectively, you have to know what each other need by way of support. And it may make a big difference to your group if you simply voice a shared concern for helping each other be your most effective selves.

Matching People With Projects

no. people: 2 to many
minimum time: 15 minutes
materials: copy of form below

One of the most important ingredients for organizational success is satisfaction. For individuals doing tasks, that means satisfaction with the jobs they're doing—a sense that the jobs are significant and that they make good use of each person's abilities. A key step in creating that sort of satisfaction is getting information about the skills and interests of group members. Here's one way to do it—the "skills bank."

Skills Bank

This approach is based on a form which could be displayed or filed for future reference, rather than used in a discussion. The form below is a sample; you might want to modify it to meet the needs of your organization. It could be filled out individually or in an interview situation. (An interviewer can encourage someone not to be modest about what they have to offer the group.)

Posting the answered forms on a bulletin board allows everyone to get an overview of the group's capabilities. Then they should be put in a file (5 x 8 card stock is a convenient format to use for the forms) and grouped according to skill categories, so that anyone can go back through them to identify resource people when a particular skill is needed.

Sample Skills Bank Form

1. Briefly describe the skills or experience you have which might be useful to the group.

_____   _____

_____   _____

_____   _____

_____   _____

_____   _____

_____   _____

To develop your list further, think about the different things which the group does. Be sure to include any skills you have in the areas of finances, media (photography, radio or TV, graphics, etc.), door-to-door surveys, setting up major events, word processing (typing, mimeo, etc.).

2. Now go back through your list and put a star beside any skill you could teach to others.

3. List any skills you would be interested in learning.

_____   _____

_____   _____

4. For good measure, list any skills or abilities which you like to use, even though they might not readily seem relevant (playing the piano, using sign language, etc.).

_____   _____

_____   _____

Deadlines and Accountability

no. people: one to several
minimum time: 5 minutes
materials: copies of form below

The best plans in the world are no good if the group lets its deadlines slide by. But also, a group that sets even a few deadlines for itself and sticks to them can feel competent and "on top of things."

1. Rate your group's ability to deal with "the deadline problem," using the form below.

DEADLINES	How I rate myself	How I rate the group
	(circle your ratings)	
able to set them:	Good Fair Poor	Good Fair Poor
able to stick to them:	Good Fair Poor	Good Fair Poor
able to hold others to them:	Good Fair Poor	Good Fair Poor

2. Compare notes with others in the group, or have someone tally the group ratings; you'll get a sense of which part(s) of the problem the group needs to work on.

3. Take five minutes or so to list some ideas for improving things; pick a few things from this list that you will try out immediately. Check back a couple of meetings later and decide whether it has helped.

Ideas for Improving Deadline Behavior

- Make sure everyone knows who's doing the job, and that person(s) can and will do it.

- Make sure each job is stated in such a way that the group will know when it's done.

- Make sure the deadline is clear; write it down, preferably on a timeline on the wall.

- Choose the best reporting pattern for your group (see sketches).

- Make sure the doer knows the consequences of not finishing (someone else is delayed, the project can't happen, etc.). Timelines can help people see the consequences of a missed deadline. ("If I don't have the addresses done by October 9, Sam can't get them typed on the 10th and Lew won't have them to the Post Office on the 12th.)

- Try to avoid frequent meetings to "discuss the accountability problem;" they may become a convenient excuse to procrastinate ("I really want to be done with this job but - - -").

- Discuss as a group what types of pressures and reminders help each individual (some respond to whip crackers, some rebel).

- Be sure people have bought into deadlines and procedures and the process of accountability.

- "External" deadlines, such as a printer's schedule, an event announced in the mass media, a date when the public expects to hear the results, can help a group get going.

Three Options for Accountability

1. Traditional Accountability -
each person reports to the same "boss."

2. Circular Accountability -
each person reports to the next person.

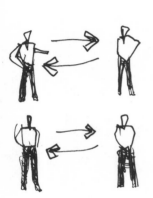

3. Pairwise Accountability -
each pair consults regularly on progress and problems.

4. Group Accountability -
each person reports to the group as a whole.

The real crunch comes when a deadline is approaching and it looks like a job won't be done on time. Who "cracks the whip?" On the job, there's the threat of being fired or perhaps of working weekends until things are done. But with voluntary citizen groups, it's very tricky. Any group that has had trouble with deadlines probably needs to spend some time with these questions:

- *Who are we accountable to—a leader, a committee, the whole organization?*

- *What inspires people to meet their deadlines—threats, reminders, sense that is matters to everyone, trust, teamwork, what?*

- *What is the best way of dealing with someone who doesn't get things done?*

- *Does the group have a tone of "it doesn't really matter if we get it done when we said"? If so what can be done to change the tune to "let's finish things up"?*

77

- How can you tell how well you're doing?

- What are some specific decisions that an evaluation can help you make?

- What kind of data could you gather to help make these decisions?

- Think about the evaluations your group has already made. What has worked best/least?

7 Evaluation

WELL...
HOW DID
WE DO??!

Many of us have heard about evaluation. It's essential for good planning or a necessary evil or just something that happens once a year, depending on who you talk to. So why bother? **Here are a few things a good evaluation can do:**

- provide information for decision making
- measure how well your group is doing to achieve its goals
- pinpoint particular activities or programs that could be improved
- help clarify "fuzzy" goals and objectives
- aid your group in planning future programs

Evaluating For What?

no. people: 3 to several
minimum time: 10 minutes
materials: newsprint, tape, felt pens

Before you rush off to design an evaluation that can do everything just mentioned, it's helpful to know why you're doing it and what's being evaluated.

This activity focuses on this as a preliminary step in evaluation design.

1. Establish the *purpose* of doing an evaluation of a fund-raising event and the *criteria* for a successful event (how you will know that the event succeeded).

2. Before the workshop or meeting begins, the facilitator should pre-pare sheets of newsprint with one of the following topics on each sheet and tape them on the walls:

   - Imagine yourself at the (auction, raffle). What would you like best/least? Why?

   - This will be a successful event if (e.g. everyone has a good time). What would be going on to indicate that this is so?

   - How will you use the information you collect from an evaluation of the event?

   - What specific decisions will it help you to make?

3. Each person in the group should then spend about five minutes jotting down her ideas about the four topics.

4. Then, spend the next five minutes in small groups discussing the ideas, checking off those items that everyone generally agrees to. (It probably will take much longer than the time allotted to reach consensus on specific criteria, for example.)

5. You should finish the exercise with a list of success criteria and a concise statement of the purpose of doing the evaluation. Now you can move on to the actual design of the evaluation.

What Would an Evaluation of "The Event" Look Like?

no. people: one to several
minimum time: 8 minutes
materials: form below

Suppose the planners wanted to find out how successful an activity was/is. Listed below are several different ways of designing an evaluation. How the evaluation is conducted usually depends on the decisions/information needed; the size and scope of the project and the energy and resources needed to conduct the evaluation.

1. Working individually, select one or more items from each column. Check these items you've selected (2 minutes).

2. Each person then shares his preferences in small groups, stating *why* the items were chosen (6 minutes).

Discussion Questions

- *Anytime you've checked one item from each of these three columns, you've identified a type of evaluation which you would presumably like to try. Look at the triplets of circles and decide, is the group really interested in gathering this information?*

- *For any evaluation information that you do want, who will be responsible for seeing that it is gathered?*

What kind of information/ data do you need to collect?	How would you do the evaluation?	When would you do the evaluation?
☐ *Behaviors*	☐ *Interviews*	☐ *Before and after*
☐ *Feelings*	☐ *Comparison group (people who didn't attend the event)*	☐ *Three weeks after*
☐ *Participation in activities*	☐ *Questionnaire*	☐ *In the middle*
☐ *Attendance*	☐ *Observation*	☐ *At the end*
	☐ *Documents (videotape, newspaper articles)*	☐ *Other*
	☐ *Physical evidence*	
☐ *Noise level*	☐ *Personal diaries of those who attended*	
☐ *Other*	☐ *Tests (attitudinal, values, etc.)*	
	☐ *Ratings by planners, those who attend, and "professional party goers"*	
	☐ *Other*	

Success Indicators

Aside from a formal evaluation process, there are usually some signals, from within and outside the organization, that will let you know how well your group is doing. These signals will vary depending on the nature and size of the program, so add your own.

Internal Indications of Success

- High member participation in decision making

- Low turnover of staff (over a reasonable amount of time)

- Fairly constant level of motivation/ energy among staff and volunteers

- Feedback from members

-

-

External Indications of Success

- Good attendance at and participation in community-wide meetings/events

- Extensive coverage in the media (not generated by the project)

- Support from politicians

- Contributions (in-kind service or monetary)

-

-

Another way to make some judgements about your group's success is to express some of your own criteria for success *prior* to starting a project.

When a program/activity is just beginning, you might want to ask all of the people who will be working on the project to write down ideas of "success signals," either individually or as a group. Then ask them, "Two years hence, how will you know that the program has succeeded?" (Will prejudice against handicapped people be entirely eliminated? Will you have recruited 222 more members?) The list of ideas can then be combined into a composite list, and individuals should be asked to rank them in order of importance. Tally up the individual responses, and review the results as a group. The list should then be kept by someone in the group (preferably in a leadership position) and reviewed periodically with all group members. Discussion should focus on those areas where little or no progress has been made. Strategies can then be adjusted *while* the program is in progress.

A Second Look at Problem Analysis

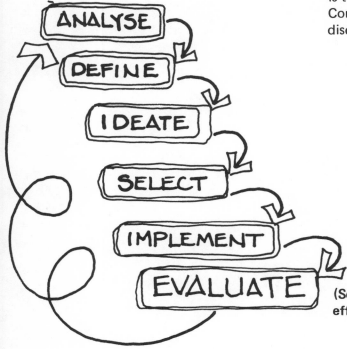

A program which has been operating for awhile provides new insights about the problem it's dealing with. So evaluation time is time to loop back to analysis and see where you stand. Consider these questions yourself or bring them up for group discussion.

- *What assumptions have been made about the nature of the problem?*

- *How well is the program working?*

- *Does it get to the root of the problem, or is it only treating the symptoms?*

- *What percent of the problem could the program eliminate, if it is fully successful?*

- *Would the problem come back on its own if the program ended?*

(See pg. 32 for discussion-criteria for evaluating root causes and effectiveness.)

A Final Note

Actual program planning often happens much more quickly than the process described in this manual. We've gone slowly through the planning process in much the same way that a piano student learns a new piece. However, the creative part of planning *can* go fast if the right idea "pops up" and everyone is happy with it. Choosing a program and timelining can go fast if there's a lot of trust and not much disagreement. But things don't always flow that smoothly. The reason we've slowed the process down is to make sure you have some "moves" you can make if the creative ideas *don't* just "pop up" or the decisions don't come easily.

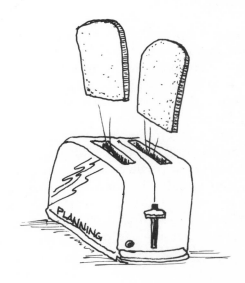

After you've spent some time with this guide and tried some of its activities, you may decide that you like the slow, step-by-step approach to planning because it allows everyone to buy into and become excited about the program. Or you may be ready to go back to "normal" planning, or—faster and less detailed—because group members grow impatient with "all talk and no action."

For us (the Citizen Involvement Training Project), the most satisfying outcome of training activities is not when specific activities are adopted by a group, but rather when a change in outlook occurs. Many organizations exist from one crisis to another in a *reactive* mode. More than one group has found itself so busy coping with crises that a new opportunity, such as selection for funding, almost a crisis too—a nuisance, one more thing to react to.

When the outlook changes to *proactive* planning—with the organization *making* waves when it chooses to and is able to see the crises as mere ripples—then a training sequence has been a success.

We envision an era in which citizen groups are increasingly able to set their own guidelines and purposes, think creatively about program options, make planning decisions with a clear sense of probable outcomes and evaluate programs with an overall awareness that planning is a necessity, not a luxury.

Satisfaction with the planning process is the best indication that we're on the right track. If the methods of citizen involvement aren't satisfying to people, they probably won't be back for more. Our *means* for planning and carrying out programs are actually our *ends* in the making, and if they aren't involving, democratic, and interesting, they will never lead us to the participatory future we envision. Our success with social change depends on our ability to implement our visions within our own organizations even as we work toward them in the outside world.

8 Resources

BOOKS

Tool Catalog—Techniques and Strategies for Successful Action Programs, American Association of University Women, 1976, 251 pp. Available from AAUW, 2401 Virginia Avenue, N.W., Washington, D.C. 20037, $6.50.

A catalog of approaches and techniques useful in planning and executing projects. Provides step-by-step processes for carrying out various techniques using low budgets and volunteers. Sections include: dealing with institutions, fact finding, publicity, information techniques, organization and planning, and demonstrations of support or opposition.

Techniques for Organizational Effectiveness, American Association of University Women, 1974, 96pp. Available from AAUW (see above), $1.95 prepaid.

A manual designed to assist in building a cohesive group and increasing group decision making skills in community projects. It correlates these areas with useful "how-to" techniques to create learning situations for improving group process.

The Universal Traveler, by Don Koberg and Jim Bagnall. Pub. by William Kauffman, 1976, 128 pp., paperback, $5.45.

A guide to problem-solving and creative thinking. Provides alternative techniques at each stage of the problem-solving process: accepting the situation, analysis, problem definition, ideation, selection, implementation, and evaluation. Abundant examples, quotations, and references.

Community Involvement in Highway Planning: A Manual of Techniques. U.S. Department of Transportation, January 1977, 360 pp. Available from the U.S. Department of Transportation, Federal Highway Administration, Office of Environmental Policy, 400 Seventh Street, S.W., Washington, D.C. 20590. Free.

Written for Department of Transportation personnel for use in encouraging and promoting citizen participation in the transportation planning process, this book would serve any citizens' group well. Three sections cover communication skills, facilitating group process and discussions, and the recorder's role at meetings. Another section concerns methods for researching the community for goals and objectives, values and priorities, local government, economic profile, social profile, nongovernmental influences, community action climate, and so on. The heart of the book concerns community involvement techniques—everything from public hearings to fishbowl planning. The complete description of over eighty different techniques includes objectives, procedures, costs, advantages, and disadvantages. References are listed for each technique, should further study be desired. The appendices include, among other things, guidelines for public meetings and workshops, guidelines for writing letters, guidelines for personal interviewing, and an audiovisual aids guidebook. A glossary, index, and bibliography are also included. Citizen groups might find this book helpful for planning. One section concerns assessing a project's level of impact on the neighborhood, local economy, environment, housing market, growth patterns, and so on. Which citizen involvement technique can best be applied to certain projects and decisions is also discussed. An amazingly clear and readable format for the depth and complexity of the material presented.

Effective Citizen Participation in Transportation Planning, by D. Jordan, S. Arnstein, J. Gray and others. U.S. Department of Transportation, 1976. Volume 1, 129 pp.; Volume 2, 298 pp. Available from the U.S. Department of Transportation, Federal Highway Administration, Social and Economic Studies Division, 400 Seventh Street, S.W., Washington, D.C. 20590. Free.

Volume 1. The first half of this book outlines the basic steps (19 in all) in the transportation planning process and identifies and provides a brief description of 37 major techniques for citizen participation, relating them to the most appropriate steps in this planning process outline. The second half of the book reviews eight case studies illustrating a single technique or combination of techniques used in various planning projects. Planning projects cited include areas other than transportation, such as construction of a dam, development of a commercial section in a large metropolitan area, and development of a regional housing policy.

Volume 2. Provided here is a detailed inventory of 37 major techniques for citizen participation, which can be used in a wide diversity of public planning programs. Among others, the techniques include advocacy planning, citizen training, neighborhood meetings, public information programs, workshops, citizen surveys, and community technical assistance. The techniques receive general description and discussion of strategy, positive and negative features, potential for resolving controversial issues, utilization in various public planning programs, costs involved, and selected bibliography for those interested in more information. A good handbook for citizen groups.

Goal Analysis, by Robert F. Mager. Fearon Publishers, 1972, 136 pp., paperback, $2.95.

A practical guide for writing useful goal statements. Includes sections on recognizing fuzzy statements, rewriting in observable terms, and testing for adequacy and completeness. Very readable.

Values Clarification, by Sidney B. Simon, Leland W. Howe, and Howard Kirschenbaum. Hart Publishing Company, 1972, 397 pp., paperback, $3.95.

Techniques for the classroom which can be easily adapted for use with citizen groups. Values clarification can provide information useful in goal-setting and program planning.

A Public Citizens' Action Manual, by Donald K. Ross. Grossman Publishers, Inc., 1973, 238 pp.; paperback, $1.95.

This is a "how-to" action manual which provides information, ideas, models, and strategies to deal with many current problems.

Will provide models for programming and ideas about the program planning process.

How To Get Things Changed: A Handbook for Tackling Community Problems, by Bert Strauss and Mary E. Stowe. Doubleday and Company, 1974, 319 pp.; $8.95.

A good book on solving local community problems from a group-centered, non-directive approach. Part One tells recent

stories of community efforts
to achieve solutions to a wide
variety of common community
problems. Part Two explains
why the authors' approach
works, and Part Three explains
the steps taken to do the job.
The third section provides
a great deal of "how-to"
information, including a
good discussion of the art
of facilitating group process
in planning and developing
conferences and meetings.

Community Problem-Solving: The Delinquency Example, by Irving A. Spergel. University of Chicago Press, 1974, 342 pp.; paperback, $3.95.

An overview both practical and
theoretical, with strategies and
steps for organizing and carrying
out community action projects.
The focus is on one issue, but the
strategies are applicable to others.

Establishment of a Long-Range Planning Capability, by S.H. Dole and others. The RAND Corporation, 1969, 107 pp.; $4.00.

This RAND study contains useful
information on the concept of
long-range planning and techniques
for integrating a planning process
into an organization.

Evaluation Research: Methods of Assessing Program Effectiveness, by Carol H. Weiss. Prentice-Hall, 1972, 160 pp.; paperback, $4.95.

Weiss explores the purposes of
evaluation, with brief
descriptions of the types of
evaluation. The focus of the
book is on ways of defining
what is being measured,
designing the evaluation, and
deciding how the data will
be used.

ORGANIZATIONS

National Center for Voluntary Action
1785 Massachusetts Ave., N.W.
Washington, D.C. 20036
(202) 467-5560

Serves as a principal national source
of information on successful
programs involving volunteers
and assists in the development
of volunteer service centers in
communities around the
nation. Services include
consultation and the collection,
analysis, and distribution of
information on various
aspects of volunteering and
volunteer management.

Write for publications lists
and annotated Reference
Lists; many are relevant to
program planning; **some are
free.**

National Information Center on Volunteerism
P.O. Box 4179
Boulder, Colorado 80306
(303) 447-0492

An organization concerned with
maximizing the effectiveness
of and involving more people
in volunteer programs and
citizen involvement efforts.
Provides technical assistance,
information services, consultation, leadership training,
and program evaluation.
Publications: Besides
information on the development,
maintenance, and evaluation of
volunteer programs, the National
Information Center on
Volunteerism has books on
running meetings and on
community change work. Send
for their publications
brochure. Their newsletter,
Voluntary Action Leadership,
is published in conjunction
with the National Center for
Voluntary Action and costs
$8 per year.

Institute for Local Self-Reliance
1717 18th Street, N.W.
Washington, D.C. 20009
(202) 232-4108

Established to investigate the
technical feasibility of
community self-reliance in
urban areas. Provides
technical assistance to muni-
cipalities and community
organizations in areas of
municipal waste management,
municipal finance,
urban energy resources,
urban food production, and
community housing. Their
publications will provide
interesting and unusual
models for program
development; send for list.

Institute for Responsive Education
704 Commonwealth Ave.
Boston, Massachusetts 02215
(617) 353-3309

Research and publication program
toward the goal of promoting
better education and more
effective involvement in educa-
tional planning. Series of very
useful booklets.

Urban Planning Aid, Inc.
Room 305/2 Park Square
Boston, MA 02116
(617) 482-6695

Provides technical assistance
and resource materials to low
income groups seeking to
improve their working and
living conditions. Aim is to
provide back-up support.
Focus is on health and safety,
media use, research (on social,
political, and economic
questions), and housing.

Cooperative Extension Service
(County offices everywhere;
state offices at land-grant
colleges and universities.)

Often, Cooperative Extension
personnel (such as 4-H workers
and Community Resource
Developers) take an interest in
the effectiveness of the citizen
organizations in their communities. They may be able to serve
as resource people themselves,
or may be able to refer a group
to others who can help with
program development and other
citizen training needs.

Citizen Involvement Training Project
Room 138 Hasbrouck Building
Division of Continuing Education
University of Massachusetts
Amherst, MA 01003
(413) 545-3450

Citizen Involvement Training Project
is publishing other training manuals
similar to this one. Also, CITP provides
workshops and consulting services
for citizen groups. See the introductory
section of this manual for more
information.